DOGS

YANN ARTHUS-BERTRAND

First published in France in 1993 by Société Nouvelle des Éditions du Chêne
Published in France in 2000 by Editions du Chêne-Hachette Livre

First published in the UK in 2000 by Cassell & Co

Reprinted 2001
Reprinted 2002
Reprinted 2003

A CIP catalogue record for this book is available from the British Library
Printed in Hong Kong

ISBN 0 304 35630 1

Art director: François Huertas
French Editors: Claire Cornubert and Joan Le Boru
English editor: Lisa Davidson
Translator: John Herrick

DOGS

YANN ARTHUS-BERTRAND

TEXT BY André Pittion-Rossillon
PHOTOGRAPHS BY Yann Arthus-Bertrand

I dedicate this book to
all those who were kind and
patient enough to come
to my studio, whether they do or
do not appear in the book.
Thank you.

PREFACE

Dogs have been a close part of mankind's life since our earliest days. As hunters, then watchdogs, sheepdogs, protectors and companions, they have chosen man just as much as man has chosen them. Each dog finds a certain sense of fulfillment performing the numerous tasks that are characteristic of its specific breed—and each breed is clearly differentiated as a result of centuries of selective breeding.

As they have a long history by our side, dogs exist only with man and through man in a bond of trust and complicity. It therefore seemed natural when Yann Arthus-Bertrand decided to depict the master and dog together. The sensitivity, the precise tone and the joy experienced by the photographer during the shoots mean that the readers of this book will enjoy the pleasure of emotion tinged with humour.

By prefacing Dogs, I feel I am perpetuating the tradition of those who set up the French Central Canine Society (CCS) one hundred and ten years ago.

Scrupulous work has meant that good representatives of some two hundred and thirty breeds have been depicted. This beautiful book, the fruit of a spontaneous idea, is also the result of teamwork. I would here like to hail my friend André Pittion-Rossillon, who wrote the texts, and to thank the breeders and owners who appear in this book for their wholehearted participation. I should also like to acknowledge the hard work of the secretaries of the CCS.

So it is in order to feel and understand better the harmony reigning between mankind and dogs, I have the pleasure of inviting you to enjoy this book.

CAMILLE MICHEL
President of the French Central Canine Society

CONTENTS

Introduction
9

INTRODUCTION

Dogs were the first animals domesticated by man. This occurred ten thousand years ago, when the two formed an alliance that enabled them to win the terrible combat for survival. During the following centuries, their relationship continued to deepen, thanks to the increasingly varied tasks dogs were given. From boundless trust, it grew into such a profound friendship that dogs now share fully in the joys and woes of the households in which they are members.

As a dog lover, Yann Arthus-Bertrand has always been fascinated by the extraordinary quality of the relationships between dogs and members of their families. This prompted him to produce a book that would depict the way dogs display their affection for their masters. He also wanted this book to help those who wished to acquire a dog to choose the companion best-suited to their lifestyle. He thus turned to the French Central Canine Society, which has been working since 1882 to improve all the breeds in France, with a request for short texts as commentaries for his photographs of each breed. All the world's recognized breeds are listed in the Society's inventory, which has been adopted by the Belgium-based World Canine Organisation (also known as the Fédération Cynologique Internationale), created in the early 1930s to develop a coherent policy concerning dog shows and dog breeding.

The breeds are classified into ten groups, according to their physical characteristics, geographical origins and dispositions. This classification has been used to structure this book because, by indicating the characteristics shared by all members of a group at the beginning of each section, long and tedious repetitions have been avoided.

The photos are amusing, moving, surprising and indicative of the special relationship between people and their dogs. Each of them is accompanied by a short text containing additional information and anecdotes.

HERDERS: SHEEPDOGS AND CATTLE DOGS

As early as prehistoric times, mankind noticed that dogs instinctively herded animals together. At first, shepherds simply took advantage of this instinct. Soon, though, they needed dogs that could help them and were adapted to the specific weather conditions and terrain where they kept their flocks or herds. By using pragmatic and carefully monitored selective breeding techniques, they created many breeds of sheepdog. A herder's work consists of two distinct tasks. The first involves taking the flock to pastures or to the pen. The dog must make certain that the sheep move in an orderly manner to facilitate the transfer. It will keep its charges on the side of the road, then form them into a line when they must cross some obstacle (such as a narrow passage, bridges, gates and so on). The dog's second job is to keep a permanent watch over the flock when it has reached the pasture, to keep the animals within their appointed limits and bring back any strays.

This demanding work requires extremely diverse capacities, notably energy, intelligence, courage, discernment and rapid reflexes. A sheepdog must also be very fit, for its job requires it to cover a considerable distance each day (from 24 to 42 miles). Finally, it must have an excellent visual memory, should only bark when strictly necessary and never bite. With the development of technological farming, shepherds made less use of their dogs. Given the wide range of skills they had learned from their previous employment, herders are today used for new forms of work: as watchdogs, searching for missing persons, detection of drugs and explosives, as guide-dogs for the blind and assistance for the disabled. It is also interesting to note that over the last few years farmers have begun to use herders again. While in the past they used to entrust them with just one species, the dogs are now expected to herd cattle, sheep, pigs and poultry. Herders form the first group in the international classification of dog breeds. This group is divided into two sub-groups: the first, "sheepdogs", contains all of those breeds used by farmers for the daily manoeu-vering and super-vision of livestock; the second, "cattle dogs," includes the breeds previously used by wholesale butchers to drive herds of animals to slaughterhouses.

All the dogs in the first group are still used in their traditional tasks. The separation into two subgroups has been maintained because of the morphological differences due to the original use of these dogs. Swiss cattle dogs are not included in the second subgroup because they are primarily mountain dogs, and are thus listed with their fellows in the second group.

BELGIAN SHEPHERD

This breed descended from various local sheepdogs that were grouped together in 1891 by Professor Reul, who held the zoology chair at the Veterinary School of Brussels. This grouping allowed him to find four dogs with the same morphology, differing only in the nature and colour of their fur. This elegant, robust, well-proportioned dog is made to withstand inclement weather and atmospheric variations. Like the German Shepherd, its ability to adapt means that it can be used for various tasks. It is about 25 inches tall, with a long head with small upright triangular ears, a slightly elongated neck and a powerful yet agile body. Vigilant and attentive, its lively, questioning stare reveals a great intelligence. It has lightning reflexes. Always on the move, it never seems to tire. It must be trained young with patience and kindness, but also with a firm hand. It requires a lot of exercise to burn off its natural energy.

MALINOIS

Its face is black, and its short fur is a black-flecked fawn colour. Exuberant and impetuous, Barox du Mas des Lavandes expresses his pleasure in carrying out the tasks that Guy Lamotte gives him by leaping into his master's arms, especially after participating in a competition.

TERVUEREN

This breed has a long black-flecked fawn or buff coat. Elda du Bois des Tôt and her four puppies (right) belong to Mrs. Chantal Jouannet.

LAEKENOIS

Of the four varieties of Belgian shepherds, this one has the fewest dogs. Its coat is rough, fawn-coloured and tousled (above, Laekenois owned by Mr. Claude Adjadj).

SCHIPPERKE

During the Middle Ages, peasants often entrusted their flocks to the breed in its native Flanders. This small, lively black Belgian devil still possesses all the qualities of a good sheepdog. With its pointed snout and small triangular ears, it looks something like a fox. It has a stocky neck, broad chest and straight back. Its abundant and resistant fur forms a beautiful black coat. The lack of a tail is characteristic. It is a rustic dog and easy to keep. Vigorous, agile and tireless, it constantly observes what is happening around it. It enjoys the company of horses. It is also a good mole hunter. It should not be forgotten that it needs a lot of exercise despite its small size. The Schipperke should receive a solid but calm training.

GROENENDAEL

This variety has a characteristic coat of long, completely black fur. Vulcain du Château des Mousseaux and Doria du Castel d'Argences (right) belong to Jean-Michel Auvray, and are excellent examples of this breed.

Below: Be-Bop du Parc de l'Aÿ, Schipperke, owned by Mrs. Pierre Marlière.

PICARDY SHEEPDOG

This is the dog that accompanied the Celts when they left southwest Germany to invade Gaul. It is average-sized, rustic yet elegant, vigorous, muscular and well built. Its face is intelligent and lively. Its medium-length wiry coat is like a Griffon terrier's. Its head is well proportioned, its neck strong and muscular and its back straight. Its coat varies from a fawn to greyish black, including all the intermediary shades, but its wiry fur, which is harsh to the touch, is never white, black, or white and black. Spontaneous and pleasant, it can be trained easily with firm but not brutal treatment. Speaking loudly is usually sufficient. It is naturally very protective of children and its master, as is shown by Vanille and Annette (preceding double page), both ready to react if anybody shows any aggression toward Vincent Diard.

BRIARD

This old French breed is a sheepdog of the plains, and its origin has never been clearly identified. Some dog specialists think it is a distant descendant of the prehistoric dog of the peat bogs, while others claim that this longhaired sheepdog came from a cross between a Barbet and a Beauce shepherd. It is longer than it is tall, and its rather elongated head is covered with long hair forming a moustache, beard and eyebrows which partly mask its eyes. Its ears are straight, its chest broad, its back straight and its rear quarters slightly curved. Its long coat looks like goat fur and requires vigorous brushing. Rustic, muscular, supple and well proportioned, it has a lively and alert appearance. Though expansive in its expressions of affection for its masters, it also enjoys lying calmly beside them, like Lukas de L'Hermitrie with Mrs. Peggy Jacoulot. This sporty dog needs activity and can tolerate life in an apartment or house only if given plenty of exercise.

BEAUCERON

This breed comes from the shorthaired variety of French flatland sheepdogs that used to be found throughout France. Rustic, solid and large (it measures from 26 to 28 inches), it is also well built and muscular. This powerful sheepdog has a long but well-proportioned head, a high broad chest, a perfectly straight back and marvellous poise. Its coat, made up of dense short hairs, is generally black and tan, though it can be harlequin (grey and black, either in equal parts or in patches). Whatever the case, all members of the breed have tan markings, particularly on the feet, hence the nickname, "red stockings." The harmonious development of its potential requires firm but not brutal training.

CATALAN SHEEPDOG

Dringola de la Folie Myosotis and Eco, (right) who belong to Mr. Emmanuel Thisse, have certain similarities with the French Pyrenean shepherd. This is not surprising, as the Catalan Sheepdog and the Pyrenean Sheepdog both come from an original breed imported from Tibet. With a maximum height of 22 inches, the Catalan shepherd has a solid head, with fine triangular ears. Its neck is muscular and short. Its long, solid body creates an impression of strength and agility. A moustache, beard and eyebrows, which do not mask its eyes, are formed by its stiff long hair, which can be straight or wavy. Its coat can be fawn, or else fawn speckled with black or grey. First and foremost a working dog, it really expresses its personality only when leading its flock. It gallops only on extremely open land and requires a lot of exercise. It can easily put up with the heat, cold or bad weather.

ABOVE: *Artus Sarah de la Mare aux Templiers, Beauceron, owned by Mr. Jacky Levilain.*

COLLIE (ROUGH)

This breed descends from the sheepdogs that escorted the Roman legions when Caesar conquered Britain. As a specialist in leading flocks of sheep, it has established itself in Scotland, where sheep are plentiful. Official recognition of this breed greatly contributed to its renown in Great Britain, where it was admired for its figure and its elegance. The collie has thus become mainly a pet, and Scottish sheep farmers often use other breeds that have retained their original rusticity and skills. Its faithfulness was popularized in the cinema by the *Lassie* films. With its graceful, exceptionally well-proportioned figure and beautiful coat, the collie's maximum height is 24 inches. It is universally admired. The natural affection which it inspires in us is increased by the characteristic softness of its gaze. Its body is long and its back straight. The tail is long and its tip turns slightly upward. Its coat is made up of dense, straight hair that is harsh to the touch. It can be fawn or somewhat flecked, black dotted with fawn, or a blue mixed with black and fawn patches. These three coats are marked with white to a greater or lesser extent.

COLLIE (SMOOTH)

A far less common smooth collie also exists. Astrellita Angel's Tears, sitting calmly beside Miss Deborah Palmer, could easily rival Lassie for her faithfulness. With great attention and tenderness, she watches over Miss Palmer's young nephews when they play, brings up the puppies of the house and washes the family's rabbit and hamsters.

ABOVE: Bella di Volorio, Collie (Rough), owned by Mr. Olivo.

GERMAN SHEPHERD

The unification of its thirty-nine states in 1870 gave rise to a strong sense of German nationalism. This inspired Captain Von Stephanitz, a Prussian officer who was a keen cynologist, to envisage the creation of a new breed which would possess all the qualities of the various regional breeds as a symbol of a united Germany. When this had been achieved, he naturally called his new breed the "German shepherd". Standing 26 inches tall, with a lean head, strong snout and straight pointed ears, this dog has firm muscles, a powerful back, a well-developed frame and solid limbs. Its thick harsh fur protects it from bad weather. This athletic dog needs plenty of daily exercise. When well-trained—it needs an inflexible but fair master—it can adapt itself to any situation. It can happily carry out any of the tasks it is given. It is also a very faithful companion and good with children.

BOUVIER DES FLANDRES

Originally from Franco-Belgian Flanders, this breed has the particularity of having a double nationality. It is thus managed by both France and Belgium. After the breeders were decimated by the violent combats which ravaged Flanders in 1914-18 and 1939-45, the French and Belgians quite sensibly worked together to re-create the breed from a handful of specimens from different pedigrees, some of which had received new crossings at the end of the nineteenth century. The huge appearance of its head is accentuated by its beard and moustache. Its short, stocky body stands on strong muscular limbs and creates an impression of great force. Its thick coat is formed of dry matte hair, which is harsh to the touch, about two inches long and slightly tousled. It is generally fawn or grey, often brindled or speckled, and sometimes plain black (right).

SCHAPENDOES

The origin of this longhaired Dutch sheepdog has not been precisely established. It is presumably the descendant of a small Asian dog that was crossed with regional Dutch dogs. Measuring a maximum of 20 inches, it is rustic, well balanced and an enthusiastic worker. Its head is covered with abundant hair, while its medium-length body has long bushy hair which is fine and dry, and forms a brown, white, black or grey coat, or any of the shades between white and black.

YUGOSLAVIAN HERDER

This Yugoslavian Herder originated in the mountains of Sar Planina, which separate Kosovo from Macedonia to the north and Albania to the north-east. Measuring an average 25 inches high, it is robust, well built, with V-shaped ears that fall down onto its cheeks. Its head is well proportioned and its body powerful and rather long. Its coat, made up of long almost flat hairs, which are rather coarse, is of one colour—any of the shades between white and a dark brown that verges on black. It requires almost no care.

The Yugoslavian Herder is better suited to country life than town, because it needs to use its energy in long trots, which is its favorite gait. Mr. Gérard Millet often says that he lives with Dimitri and his partner rather than the other way round. By this provocative statement, he shows that he has trained his two Sarplaninacs so well that they have become full-fledged members of the family.

ABOVE: Fenouille de la Vallée des Troglodytes, Schapendoes, owned by Mrs. Claude Couprie.

POLISH LOWLAND SHEEPDOG

It was only when the new classification by the World Canine Organisation was adopted in 1990 that this name was given to the Polish Shepherd, which used to be called the Valley Shepherd. As for dog-breeders, they use the term "Nizinny." Like most European sheepdogs, part of its ancestry is to be found in primitive Asian sheepdogs. Its head is covered with bushy hair on the forehead, cheeks and chin. Measuring 20 inches, its body is longer than it is tall, with a flat, highly muscular back and oblique rear quarters. Its fur is long, thick and dense. It can be any colour. Eliaska and Comte, known as Droopy Z Doliny (preceding double page), who belong respectively to Miss Patricia Noël and Mrs. Christa Lochner, are incapable of resisting the attraction of a tennis ball, especially when thrown by children, their favourite playmates.

KOMONDOR

At a height of 32 inches, this is Hungary's tallest sheepdog. Its ancestors were middle-sized primitive Asian dogs that accompanied the Mongols when they invaded Hungary in 1241. Its large head is like a ball of fur that sticks out in perfect proportion from its square, slightly oblong body. Its low tail hangs straight down. Its form is readily recognizable thanks to its thick coat of long white rope-like hairs, which tend to knot and become matted. Distant, independent and dominant, it needs careful upbringing, like the one given to Szentmiklôsi-Kéktavi Érzö by Mr. Dominique Montois who, in return, is lavished with affection. With its strong constitution, the Komondor is a rural dog which is unsuited to life in an apartment. It is extremely resistant because in its country of origin it was accustomed to living outdoors, whatever the weather.

PULI

The ancestors of this Hungarian dog, with a maximum height of 18 inches, were the primitive Asian dogs that accompanied nomads on their travels. It probably arrived in Hungary with the Magyars at the end of the ninth century. It is solid, lean and very muscular. Its body, which forms almost an exact square, is entirely covered by long shaggy fur, which is uniform in colour and wavy. It tends to become matted so that, when young, it can look like a Komondor. Its coat can be plain black, a reddish black, grey or white. Szegvarréti-Al-Palis (right), aged eleven, adores music like his master Mr. Imre Horvath. He has a wide musical taste. He enjoys listening to the overture of Carmina Burana so much that he gives off a song-like bark.

ABOVE: Bundas de la Bacska, Puli, owned by Mrs. Chagnard.

Breeders have not yet developed a precise hypothesis concerning this dog's origins. All we know is that its ancestors lived in the Crimea between the Black Sea and the Sea of Azov. At 26 inches, it has a long head with small dangling triangular ears. Its back is straight and very strong. Its coat consists of long, thick, coarse hair that is bushy and slightly wavy, generally white but occasionally white and yellow, white flecked with grey or any shade of grey. Rather undemanding, it can adapt to any weather conditions.

Guella, known as Pluschka, with her paws lovingly on Mrs. Claudine Ducret, is one of the only three of this breed presently living in France. Her mistress is always proud of the admiration she receives whenever she participates in a dog show.

DUTCH SHEPHERD

This dog measures no more than 25 inches tall, and has a morphology similar to the Belgian Shepherd. Not a surprising fact since it is the product of crossing local Dutch dogs and Malinoises. Its head is of average length and topped with straight ears. Its body is powerful and its back short, straight and strong. The first specimens of this breed appeared in France in the 1980s. Eros du Domaine des Crocs Sanglants (preceding double page), who belongs to Miss Sophia Anastassiades, has made a good start as a guard dog. He belongs to a common short-haired variety. Although the coat is wiry, it is not too short and can be brown, yellow or ginger, brindled with gold or silver. There are two other varieties:

• a wirehaired coat which is rather harsh to the touch, with few or no wavy hairs;

• or a coat with long, flat and harsh fur.

BERGAMASCO

This breed descends from Asian mastiffs crossed with local dogs from the province of Bergamo, in northern Italy. As is shown by Usmina dell'Albera, who belongs to Mrs. Maria Andreoli, this middle-sized sheepdog's upper body is covered by abundant, extremely long hair, which is resistant and coarse, while on the lower body it forms long hanging tresses. This gives it a similar look to Hungary's Komondors and Pulis. Its coat is generally grey, but can also have patches of all shades between grey and black. More rarely, it can also be black with a scattering of white patches. It is rustic, robust and well proportioned.

PYRENEAN SHEEPDOG (LONG-HAIRED)

This French breed certainly descends from the Tibetan terrier, whose descendants accompanied the Suevians when they invaded Gaul under Ariovista. Established in the high valleys of the Pyrenees in Bigorre, they remained there until the late nineteenth century, which helped them remain pure. There are two varieties with the same morphological characteristics. The "longhaired" variety has abundant fur, which is "brushed up" on its cheeks and the sides of its snout. The body is lean, the back short and the hindquarters oblique. The coat can be fawn, as with Torquade de l'Estaube, grey or harlequin. Its lively features and great vivacity of movement give it a highly characteristic appearance. Given its rather pugnacious nature, it needs a firm yet skilful master. It is a rural dog that needs plenty of exercise.

PYRENEAN SHEEPDOG (SMOOTH-FACED)

The second variety has short hair on the face, is slightly larger and has fine short hair on the head, as well as a slightly longer muzzle. Florac du Val Soannan and First du Val Soannan (right), flanking David Reilhac, are excellent examples.

ABOVE: Torquade de l'Estaube, Pyrenean Sheepdog, owned by Mrs. Claudine Brault.

SHETLAND SHEEPDOG

The Shetland Isles, to the north of Scotland, contain numerous flocks of sheep. To guard them, the shepherds imported collies from the mainland and Nordic dogs from Iceland. Crossing them resulted in the Shetland. At 15 inches, this sheepdog looks like a miniature collie. Its form is harmonious, with a long head topped with small ears, a muscular neck and a long body with a straight back. As a working dog, it can tolerate bad weather and has beautiful fur consisting of long, straight, stiff hair. It can be fawn flecked with black, black with fawn markings, or blue with black markings. There can be some white on its chest, throat, limbs or the tip of its tail, except if the coat is black and tan, in which case there is not the slightest trace of white. Its coat can also be black and white—which is extremely rare in France.

AUSTRALIAN CATTLE DOG

This breed was created in the second half of the nineteenth century by Australian breeders who wanted a dog capable of leading flocks over the immense territories they had to cover. A result of crossing dingos (tamed by the Aborigines) with European sheepdogs, this is a strong, compact working dog, full of stamina and extraordinary power. Its head is topped with upright slightly pointed ears. Its body is longer than it is tall—it measures a maximum 20 inches—with a strong horizontal back. Its smooth, wiry fur, which lies flat, is well suited to protecting it against bad weather conditions. Its coat is either blue, like Gribouille de la Bakia, owned by Laurence Courfin, sometimes with black, blue or tan patches on the head, or a speckled red with occasionally dark red markings on the head.

44

ABOVE: Shetland Sheepdog, owned by Mrs. Catherine Lecomte.

This dog's descriptive name says it all. Its ancestors were the Roman sheepdogs that arrived in Britain with Caesar's legions. Its fur often leads beginners to mistake it for an Old English sheepdog, even through the latter is stronger and has a shortened tail, while the Bearded collie's tail reaches the bend of its knees. Of an average size—22 inches at most—it is quite long and, despite its solid build, not very heavy. The hair on the dog's head becomes longer as it reaches the chest, thus forming the characteristic beard which gives it its name. Its straight, wiry, abundant fur must never be brushed. Its coat can be different colors: black, grey, brown, blue or beige with or without white markings. The Bearded collie has a working dog's temperament: alert, curious, lively and active. It detests solitude. It is extremely sporty, merry and frisky.

Right: Clovis du Kastell a Labous Mor with Mrs. Françoise Pouliquen.

SAARLOOS WOLFDOG

In about 1920, a Dutch dog-lover called Saarloos decided to create a new breed of sheepdog by crossing a she-wolf and an Alsatian. Aware of the considerable difficulties he would face, he consulted some geneticists. After his work had been interrupted by World War II, he started again in the 1950s. He died before completing his project. Fortunately, the Dutch national cynophile association took over, and the breed was recognized in 1975, when it was considered to be stable. This large dog, which can measure as much as 30 inches, is longer than it is tall, powerful, and looks like a wolf. It has wiry, straight hair, providing a coat that can vary between light and dark black, light to dark brown, or from light cream to white. The master must be kind and extremely patient, given this breed's independent tendencies.

MAREMANER HERDER DOG

The distant ancestors of this breed were the Asian mastiffs that accompanied the Mongols to Europe in the middle of the thirteenth century. These mastiffs were then crossed with local dogs from the Abruzzi region (in central Italy) and from Maremma (by the Tyrrhenian Sea). It can reach 29 inches, is powerfully built and, with its rustic yet distinguished appearance, is a beautifully vigorous dog. Its head is like that of a white bear. Its body is covered with long, abundant coarse hair, sometimes slightly wavy, of a plain white colour yet occasionally with a very small number of ivory, bright orange or lemon yellow markings. This athletic dog must not be confined in a small space. Dandalo de la Vallée Macchia is absolutely uncompromising when he stands guard on Mr. Mario Massuci's property.

ABOVE: Naima Belladonna de Louba-Tar, Saarloos Wolfdog, owned by Mrs. Souquière.

WELSH CORGI

In Great Britain, this Welsh dog is considered to be the descendant of primitive dogs that arrived there with the Celts several centuries B.C. However, it seems rather to have been product of crosses between local Welsh dogs with the Visigoths' spitz (Västgötaspets) which went with the Vikings during their raids on the English coast during the eighth and ninth centuries. Very short (12 inches), it has great vigour and stamina, is a hard worker and is always in action. Its head makes it look like a fox, and it has rather large ears. Its body is long and powerful. This breed has two varieties.

WELSH CORGI PEMBROKE

This breed has only a tiny stub of a tail, and its coat consists of average-length straight hair, which is never soft, wavy or very harsh. Left: Pemland Music Masters, Venwoods Gambling Man and Blackbird de la Caverne des Anges, owned by Mrs. Jocelyne Thomas.

WELSH CORGI CARDIGAN

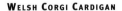

This dog's wiry short- or medium-length fur forms a coat that can be any colour, with or without white streaks, provided white does not dominate. Its tail is of average length.

OLD ENGLISH SHEEPDOG

The name of this dog comes from the fact that it an extremely old breed, derived from Roman sheepdogs crossed with other dogs from the continent at the end of the seventeenth century. Many breeders have come up with other hypotheses, but all lovers of this breed agree that its ancestors were longhaired sheepdogs. Since its official name is rather long, the British have given it a nickname based on its physique—the bobtail. Measuring 22 inches on average, it is a strong dog with a compact but well-proportioned appearance. It is covered with wiry hair, which is not straight but shaggy. Its coat is grey or blue, with or without white markings. Stocky and muscular, Tottel Free Mason at Ebonyivory and her daughter Ivory's Georgia Brown, who pose quietly beside Mr. and Mrs. Claude Ritter (right), amble along like all bobtails when they are in action. They trot by simultaneously lifting and dropping the limbs on one side. The resulting sway is rather reminiscent of the gait of a bear.

ABOVE: Droupy of Saint-Hilaire's Park, Welsh Corgi Cardigan, owned by Mrs Maurice Boulon.

TATRA SHEPHERD

This large Polish dog standing at 28 inches is the product of crosses between Polish mastiffs and dogs from the Carpathian mountains in the Tatras region on the border of Poland and Czechoslovakia. The fact that this region remained isolated until the end of the nineteenth century greatly contributed to the breed's purity, better known as the "sheepdog of the Tatras." Its head, with a strong and relatively pointed snout, has rather thick medium-length triangular ears level with its eyes. With its long, bulky, compact body it gives off a strong impression of power and vitality. The fur on its head is short and dense, while the fur on its body is thick, long, harsh to the touch, straight or slightly wavy, creating a sturdy plain white coat.

KUVASZ

Its great height—up to 30 inches—makes this Hungarian dog look both powerful and noble. Its long head is topped with high ears, which flop down next to the scalp. Its body is long, and its hindquarters somewhat drooping. Its tail, which points down to its knees, is straight as far as its tip. Its coat consists of white, medium-length coarse hair, which is wavy and slightly stiff. Full of stamina, it can trot effortlessly for 15 to 20 miles. Mrs. Elisabeth Agnoux brought Portam Öre Döllar from Hungary when he was just seven weeks old. He has adapted perfectly to his life in France. He has been watching carefully over Mrs. Agnoux's daughter for the last three years.

ABOVE: Fully du Pic du Roc Blanc, Podhale, owned by Mr. Christian Cerf.

KELPIE

This noble Australian sheepdog's solid muscular frame and flexible limbs give it enormous stamina. Mr. Patrick Lusso, a biologist in Nouméa, took advantage of a trip to France to exhibit Goofy du Domaine de Ouassio at several European dog shows. This breed is the result of a cross between Scottish sheepdogs imported to Australia in 1870 and a local bitch, a descendant from the collies that had accompanied the first European settlers. This bitch was called Kelpie, and her name was given to the breed, which was officially recognized at the beginning of the twentieth century. The kelpie is between 18 and 20 inches tall, and its head is topped with straight medium-length pointed ears, rather like a fox. Its neck is strong, its hindquarters long and drooping. Its coat, consisting of a double set of hard, stiff hair, can be tan, red, red and tan, or chocolate and blue. Lively and enthusiastic, this remarkable sheepdog is docile and devoted.

BORDER COLLIE

This breed is the result of crosses made in the Middle Ages between various breeds of British sheepdogs, which themselves descended from Roman dogs. The word "border" in its name comes from the fact that sheep breeders in the borderlands between Scotland and England were so taken by its courage, stamina and sway over a flock that they adopted it as their favorite sheepdog. Of modest height—about 21 inches—this rustic dog has a fine long head, a strong muscular neck, with a rather long body and powerful broad back. Its coat consists of dense hair of an average texture, which can be any colour. The transformation of this collie into a household pet has made it even more appreciated as a sheepdog, since it has lost none of its rural nature. In France, the Border Collie Association, which manages the technical running of the breed under the direction of the Central Canine Society, intends to maintain it only in its role of a working dog. Mr. Antoine Brimbœuf, a shepherd in Rambouillet, greatly appreciates Dan. This three-year-old border collie's help is essential to him when he takes his large flock on its daily manoeuvres.

AUSTRALIAN SHEPHERD

This dog is the result of crosses between quite large Basque sheepdogs, which accompanied the first Basque shepherds that emigrated to Australia in the nineteenth century. These enthusiasts nicknamed it "Aussie". This breed still has not been recognized either by the Australian Kennel Club, or the American Kennel Club, where many specimens can be found. Until the World Canine Organisation officially recognizes this breed, none of its members can be inscribed in the genealogical pedigree books of its member countries. It is a medium-sized sheepdog, which can reach a height of 23 inches.

PORTUGUESE SHEEPDOG

This dog belongs to a very old breed, whose origins have never been precisely identified. But its indubitable similarities with the French Pyrenean Sheepdog and the Catalan Spaniel makes it seem likely that its ancestors were also primitive dogs from Tibet. Thanks to Agnès do Picoto dos Barbados, posing here with Mr. Francisco Correa-Cordoso, we can see that this longhaired sheepdog is of average size. It is 19 inches tall, with a strong broad head and a rather short snout. Its high ears dangle down. Its prominent chest is ample, while its hindquarters are slightly drooping. Its long smooth fur has the same consistency as goat's hair and gives its face a beard, whiskers and long eyebrows. Its coat is yellow, brown, grey, fawn or yellow-dun. It has a rustic appearance and is lively, devoted and watchful.

ABOVE: Australian Shepherd, owned by Mrs. Brigitte Joly and Mrs. Marie-Anne Bernard.

PINSCHER AND SCHNAUZERS
MOLOSSIANS
SWISS MOUNTAIN AND CATTLE DOGS

Although all dogs, even lap dogs, instinctively try to protect "their" territory by alerting their masters as soon as an intruder tries to force his way in, not all of them are suited to the job. A guard dog must, of course, sound the alarm when it detects something wrong, but it should do so only when really necessary. A good guard dog must combine a cool head with great vigilance, good judgement and an ability to dissuade the intruder. When necessary, a guard dog must incapacitate the intruder without hurting him or, at least, hold him down until its master is in control of the situation. Finally, it must have great physical prowess and stamina, qualities necessary to guard an isolated house and, even more so, a large property. The dogs possessing these qualities have been assembled in the first section of the second group: the pinschers and the schnauzers. For many years, flocks were decimated by various predators (wolves, bears, jackals, pumas, jaguars and lynxes). To protect them, shepherds used powerful dogs that lived permanently with their charges and had just one mission: to protect them from attack. Shepherds today don't fear such ferocious predators, but they have new threats, such as stray dogs. These are generally dogs that have been abandoned; they have returned to an almost wild state and live together in packs like wolves. Many flocks have fallen victim to such attacks, and shepherds are increasingly reintroducing protection dogs in their flocks. Such use remains relatively limited, however, and flock protection dogs are most often used as guard dogs, like those in the first section. Yet their particular morphology justifies the creation of a second section in the second group, the "Molossians." These dogs have powerful snouts, drooping ears, bulky heads and bodies, a thick skin that is sometimes loose, and are rather tall. This is not surprising because to oversimplify, they all have a common ancestor—a primitive Asian mastiff. After the last floods of the Quaternary era, the falling water level encouraged Tibetan tribes to leave their high plateaus along with their primitive mastiffs and gradually to travel as far as the Middle East. Tibetan mastiffs were thus the forefathers of the large Assyrian mastiffs that were so highly reputed in days gone by. Later, other migrants left Assyria with their mastiffs and headed for the Mediterranean. They colonized Greece and Italy, then gradually moved into the Balkans, Germany, the

Iberian peninsula, Scandinavia and the British Isles. Such waves of migration also moved in the opposite direction. Nomads from Tibet moved into Southeast Asia, across China and then, having crossed the Bering Straits, filtered down into the interior of North America. Thus, after crossings with local dogs, the primitive Asian mastiffs are the forefathers of all of the breeds in the subgroup "Molossians." Finally, although Swiss cattle dogs all have mountain dog characteristics and can protect flocks, they can also lead and watch them, just like sheepdogs.

PINSCHER

The ancestor of this German dog was the famous dog of the Neolithic peat bogs, which became the companion of hunters and fishermen living on the North Sea coast. As the centuries passed, the descendants of this dog divided into two branches, which are differentiated only by the nature of their fur; the pinschers descend from the shorthaired variety. Of average height, it has a robust head tipped with vertical ears, a square body and a highly-placed docked tail. Its short thick shiny fur forms a coat that can be either uniform (from brown to fawn) or else of two colours (black with red or brown markings). Etex de la Capellière, who belongs to Mr. Gaudfroy, amply displays the elegance of these lively, energetic dogs, which are not great barkers. There is also a variety of miniature Pinscher, which is different for its size (10 to 12 inches instead of 17 to 19 inches on average) and by an additional coat colour (brown or greyish blue with brown markings).

DOBERMANN PINSCHER

This breed was created in Germany and appeared in Apolda, near Erfurt in Thuringen, in the second half of the nineteenth century. It owes its existence to Frederick Ludwig Dobermann, who created it by means of a series of empirical crossings, which he kept secret. From its morphology, it probably has pinscher blood, but the other elements remain unknown—pointer, mastiff, beauceron or greyhound? It doesn't really matter, for the result is what really counts. The Dobermann is rather tall, with a powerful muscular frame, a harmonious line and natural elegance heightened by its haughty demeanour and resolute expression. It is easy to understand why little Mylène Lecoq so admires the protection of Ertog Erphun von Rauberstolz. The Dobermann's head is like a long sectioned cone. It is finely sculpted, and its ears are highly placed and erect. Its back is short and firm, and its legs extremely straight. Its short thick rough fur forms a shiny coat that is black and tan, chestnut brown and tan, or blue and tan. It needs a firm, fair master who gives it enough exercise to satisfy its enormous energy.

AFFENPINSCHER

Despite its small size, this lively dog makes a good guard dog, adapting well to life in an apartment. It is part of the Pinscher group because it, too, descends from the dogs of the peat bogs. The Germans named it because of its appearance, its abundant stiff fur, its vivacity and especially its ape-like face ("Affenpinscher" means "monkey terrier"). As Diva de la Rochardière watches, Duck de la Rochardière poses in front of the white backdrop that Mrs. Dominique Laporte is holding to set off the purity of his black coat.

SCHNAUZER

Like the Pinscher, its ancestors were the dogs of the peat bogs, but the Schnauzer is part of the longhaired branch. This explains why, other than the difference of appearance due to their fur, there is a great similarity between these two German breeds. The Schnauzer is characterized by its beard and bushy eyebrows, which give it a quadrangular appearance, and its thick wiry fur. Its high energy level means that it needs plenty of daily exercise. There are three different-sized varieties. The two coat colours, black, and salt and pepper, can be found in the three varieties; the miniature Schnauzers have two extra coat colours, black and silver, which is greatly valued, and white, which despite its rarity is considered to be a minor factor.

STANDARD SCHNAUZER

This dog stands between 18 and 20 inches tall, which means it can comfortably live in an apartment. Preceding double page: left, Hweeko Rivale-Tiffany, who belongs to Mrs. Dominique Schall-Marx; right, Mrs. Jeannette Seltz's Mihan Finland Prinsess is the first Finnish Schnauzer to be imported into France.

MINIATURE SCHNAUZER

Between 12 and 14 inches tall, this alert dog is good at giving warnings. Mr. and Mrs. Peeters' Dylan de la Croix de Vilpert (right) is a musician. When their grand-daughter plays the flute, he "sings" by barking in time.

GIANT SCHNAUZER

Measuring from 24 to 28 inches, rustic, powerful, fast and full of stamina, this is an ideal dog for protecting large properties. Brahms de Monlaur (right) has great sympathy for small animals. While Mr. Laurent Rabaté was having lunch, a yapping Brahms arrived, then pulled him over two hundred yards to help a small cat that was lying wounded in a cornfield.

BULLDOG

A descendant of the mastiff, the British bulldog was one of the stars of the old-time dogfights. When these were outlawed, interest in this breed declined. It was saved by British breeders who worked on producing a dog that was lighter but still as bulky. The modern breed of bulldog was established at the end of the nineteenth century. It has an extremely short face and a broad snub nose. Its limbs are athletic and its body well made. Its coat consists of short, thick, smooth fur that is either uniform red, "sooty" (uniform with a black mask or snout) or a mixture of white and red. This dog has a delightful temperament belied by its severe appearance. Following double page: Crazy Horse de Wounded Knee and Boo's Apple Cider love playing with the garbage can lid, which they vigorously drag around Mrs. Céline Bottussi's garden.

BULLMASTIFF

During the second half of the nineteenth century, important British landlords became alarmed by the huge amount of game that was being poached. So they asked dog breeders to create a dog that could trap poachers and hold them down until the gamekeeper arrived. This was successfully done by crossing mastiffs and British bulldogs, hence the name of the breed. Its body is large and square, its head high with a short snout. Its V-shaped ears are highly placed and wide apart. Its chest is broad and high, its back short and straight. Its hind legs are powerful and straight, while its front legs are strong and muscular. It is well protected against the weather by its short wiry fur, which can be any shade of brindled fawn or red. Standing from 25 to 27 inches tall, it weighs between 110 and 130 pounds. It is solid, active, hard-working, faithful, strong and vigilant. Right: M. Jean-Pierre Guillemet et Édouard de Molossie.

BOXER

The distant ancestors of this breed are the mastiffs that were used as dogs of war. But this German breed came into being in 1890 after a German dog, the "Bullenbeisser" (bull biter), which has now disappeared, was crossed with a British bulldog. Measuring on average 24 inches and weighing in at about 65 pounds, this great athlete has a short black snout, vertical pointed ears and a muscular body. Its short shiny fur makes for a coat that is either uniformly fawn or has darker stripes. The boxer has the supple gait of a well-trained athlete. It needs plenty of exercise. Because of its enthusiasm, impetuousness and speed, it must be kept on a leash when taken for walks. Following double page: *"Quo non ascendet?"* Patrick Marizy seems to be thinking as he contemplates Clovis des Plaines du Nord. Fouquet's proud motto in fact perfectly fits this mascot for the advertisements of Kleber-Colombes tyres.

GREAT DANE

When the Alani invaded Europe at the end of the second century, they came with impressive mastiffs that were used as dogs of war, and continued to be used as such until the Middle Ages. Later, these powerful mastiffs were crossed with Irish greyhounds, and the Great Dane was born. Despite its large size—it stands at over 32 inches—the robust Great Dane is very well proportioned. Ephèbe des Terres de la Rairie (right), who belongs to Mrs. Vaslin-Soron, has the long expressive head that is so characteristic of great Danes —pendulous chops, a snout finishing vertically and ears cut into a point. A firm yet gentle upbringing brings out the Great Dane's inborn good nature.

NEAPOLITAN MASTIFF

This is Italy's national guard dog
descends from Assyrian ma
introduced to Italy
Phoenicians. The Romans
a dog of war, and also to
one of their circus s
large and short, con
jaws well develo
and triangular
in its neck
straight
The
sm

It
...stiffs
...the
...used it as
...rned into
...ars. Its head is
...ered with folds, its
...ped and its ears short
...Its skin forms dewlaps
...its front and back legs are
...nd its hindquarters oblique.
...ur is short, dense, thin and
...oth. The coat can be black, grey,
...ahogany or fawn. Wherever and
whenever he goes out, Mr. Patrick
Salomon knows that he is in no
danger while he is with Arno de la
Fouinerie, whose fierce looks and
imposing size are extremely dissuasive.

The Shar Pei descends from now-extinct Chinese mastiffs. The provinces of Kuang-si and Kuang-tong, by the south China Sea, were the cradle of this breed. It nearly disappeared when Mao Tse Tung decided to eliminate all dogs because they deprived people of food. Fortunately, some mainland Chinese took refuge in Taiwan in 1949 with their dogs. Then, during a study tour to Tai-lai, some American breeders discovered the Shar Pei, decided to save the breed and, with that in mind, acquired several males, which they took back to America. While presenting Gabin des Roses de Porcelaine, Mrs. Cécile Aleman emphasizes a few typical characteristics of this breed: the many fine wrinkles that cover its forehead and cheeks, forming long folds, the small thick triangular ears, the folds covering the body, and the thick tail that is round at its base and finishes in a point. It is a pity that he is not showing his bluish-black tongue. Standing 16 to 20 inches tall, it has very short bristly fur, harsh to the touch, and a black, tan, dark brown, beige or cream coat. Despite its sad appearance, it is in fact a good-natured dog. It used to be the great star of dogfights in China. Right: Mrs. Simone Bernier's Dollar.

DOGUE DE BORDEAUX

Mr. Michel Guignard's Eros de l'Etang de Mirloup displays the typical head of a Dogue de Bordeaux—low, large, trapezoidal and furrowed with wrinkles—as well as the bull-like neck. The Dogue de Bordeaux descends from the mastiffs that the Alani left in southwest Gaul when the Huns pushed them into Spain. When crossed with other local dogs, these mastiffs created the Aquitaine mastiff that later, during the nineteenth century, became France's national dog under its present name. The losses that breeders experienced during the two world wars were so great that the breed almost disappeared. It was saved by the determination of the breeders who, led by Professor Triquet, adopted rigorous but efficient methods of selection.

The Dogue de Bordeaux is a thick-set, muscular colossus. His coat, made up of fine short soft fur, is plain mahogany or fawn.

MASTIFF

Like all mastiffs, the affection that Dogessa du Domaine du Cataou, who belongs to Mrs. Michelle Premat, shows her masters is as great as her weight. The modern mastiff is the descendant of the great mastiffs that accompanied the Celts when they colonized Britain, several centuries before Christ. This dog, which is England's national mastiff, is large, powerful and impressive, yet also well proportioned and well built. Its skull is long and wide, with a snub snout, a very broad lower jaw, a high large chest and an extremely muscular back. Its fur is short, flat against the body and fawn-coloured.

DOGO ARGENTINO

The ancestors of Elton du Chêne le Gué, presented by Mr. Roberto di Blasi, were the dogs of war that accompanied Diaz de Solis when he landed near the Rio de la Plata. The descendants of these mastiffs were highly prized for dogfights. To make them even more ferocious, they were crossed with Cordova mastiffs, a non-extinct breed. They soon became uncontrollably aggressive. Then, in the early twentieth century, Mr. Antonio Nores Martinez decided to create a breed capable of hunting the wild boars that damaged his crops and the pumas that massacred his livestock. He crossed the ferocious local mastiffs with Great Danes, pointers and Irish greyhounds, and established the modern Dogo Argentino in 1930. Though less elegant and smaller, this dog is reminiscent of the Great Dane. It has short-cropped ears, a thick neck and extremely muscular limbs. Its coat consists of rather coarse, short hairs and is uniformly white. It has a well-balanced personality.

ABOVE: Dogessa du Domaine du Cataou, Mastiff, owned by Mrs. Michelle Premat.

ROTTWEILER

This breed is the result of crosses between mastiffs used as dogs of war by the Roman legions, and dogs from the region around Rottweil, a town near Stuttgart. Exy du Trou du Diable, who belongs to Mr. Gilles Garnier, is a good example of the breed, with a medium build and a compact, vigorous stature. Her rusticity is combined with harmonious lines. The head, of medium length, is topped with dangling ears that hang towards the front. The neck is firm and powerful, the rib cage large and the hindquarters broad. The legs are straight and widely placed. The black and tan coat consists of average length fur, which is smooth and dense. The Rott-weiler trots along vig-orously, taking long strides.

FILA BRASILEIRO

When Alvares Cabral's comrades landed in Brazil in 1500, they were accompanied by Portuguese Mastiffs. In the seventeenth century, the planters used their descendants to hunt down runaway slaves. Crossed with indigenous dogs, these mastiffs produced the Fila Brasileiro, which turned out to be very good at protecting flocks against jaguars. It has now become Brazil's police dog. Standing between 26 and 30 inches tall and weighing at least 110 pounds, it has a robust frame, longer than it is tall, with a thick hide and a tail that ends in a point. Although the coat may be of any colour, brindled fawn is the most common. Kama amazes Mrs. Marie-Pierre Fournier with his dexterity. He opens the garden door, then closes it behind himself when wants to come inside. When he is thirsty, he goes to the bathroom and manages to turn on the tap in the bidet all by himself.

ABOVE: Exy du Trou du Diable, Rottweiler, owned by Mr. Gilles Garnier.

ATLAS SHEPHERD

The precise origin of this Moroccan dog is still unknown, but it is certain that it comes from the upper Atlas Mountains, where shepherds used it to protect their flocks against jackals. This rustic dog is remarkably powerful and mobile. Its head makes it look like a bear, while its back gives it a slightly plunging profile. Its hind legs are straight with muscular thighs, and its tail is long and bushy. The coat consists of very thick hair, about 2 inches long, which is good protection from both heat and cold. It is fawn, sandy, white and fawn, white and black, or tricoloured. Dr. Id Sidi Yahia is justly proud to present Jaoui, who belongs to Mr. Ben Youssef. Jaoui has the strength and vivacity of his breed, as well as its extraordinary obedience.

CAUCASIAN SHEPHERD

Originally from the mountainous region that extends from the Black Sea to the Caspian Sea, this powerful Russian dog stands 26 inches tall. Thanks to the inaccessibility of the valleys of the Caucasus, the breed has remained extremely pure. It is strong, weighs about 110 pounds, and has beautiful fur—which can be of any length. This calm dog has a highly developed protective instinct. Hypteck (right), for example, found it strange that electricians were walking back and forth in front of Mr. and Mrs. Olivier's house. He leapt over the fence and forced them to climb up some telephone poles, where they remained until Mr. Olivier returned.

TIBETAN MASTIFF

The largest population of this breed can now be found in Nepal. The history of this dog parallels that of the tribes living in the mountains of Tibet. As well as protecting herds of yaks, it also guarded colonies of llamas. Despite its respectable size, the modern Tibetan Mastiff is smaller than the original Mastiff, which is the ancestor of all of the Molossians. Its large noble head is topped with small dangling ears. Its shoulders and neck are covered with long, wiry fur, with a thick under-fur forming a mane. Its coat can be black, black and tan, grey, grey and tan or fawn. It stands at a minimum of 26 inches and has a supple gait and a tail that curls over its back. Following double page: Djouley de la Tour Chandos is a descendant of the first Tibetan Mastiff to be imported into France. Mr. Jacques Thomas is still amazed to see him sleep on his back with his paws in the air.

LEONBERGER

There are two different hypotheses explaining the origin of this breed. Some people say it descends from a large seventeenth-century Austrian mountain dog and, thanks to its proud muscular stature and the beauty of its coat, was nicknamed the "lion of the mountains" (the meaning of "Leonberg"). Others think the breed was created by crossings between Newfoundlands, Pyrenean mountain dogs and Saint Bernards, carried out near Leonberg, a town in southwest Germany. The Leonberger is a big dog—29 to 32 inches tall—with a muscular, well-proportioned body, topped by a rather thin head with flat dangling years. Its coat consists of abundant, smooth flat fur. It can be semi-smooth or coarse, and sometimes slightly wavy. Its coat is generally fawn with a black mask. This large dog does not drool. It hates solitude and loves to dig.

NEWFOUNDLAND

It is generally thought that this dog's ancestors were Assyrian Mastiffs taken to Newfoundland by the Vikings. It was introduced to France in the late nineteenth century by French cod fishers, who were won over by its good nature. It stands at about 28 inches and weighs about 140 pounds. Its huge head is topped by small ears, set back. Its back is straight, and its tail of moderate length. Its coat can be jet black or brown; it consists of a double layer of flat, dense, coarse fur, which is oily and impermeable. The pose that Mr. Etienne Engrand has adopted behind Van Het Hooigueen is intended to show how, despite its great strength, the Newfoundland has never been a dangerous guard dog; in addition, it has a history of saving drowning people.

ABOVE: Dagobert du Ruisseau de Corseilles, Leonberger, owned by Mrs. Anne-Marie Paris.

Serra da Estrela mountain dog

This descendant of a large Asian
Mastiff, which probably arrived in
Portugal on a Phoenician boat, made
its home in the centre of the country
in the mountains of the Serra Estrela.
It stands between 26 and 29 inches,
weighs from 90 to 110 pounds, is
rustic, broad-backed and gifted with
great vivacity. Its long head has small
drooping triangular ears. The back is
short and almost horizontal. The tail is
shaped like a scimitar. The fawn or
wolf-grey coat can be uniform,
speckled or mottled. In the past, it was
often used for dragging carts up the
steep tracks in the region. It is very
docile, which explains why Derby
d'Ayriana-Vaedja, here accompanied
by Mr. Laplante, wins many prizes in
agility competitions, as well as in dog
shows, thanks to his training with Mrs.
Christiane Laplante.

SAINT BERNARD

When the Roman legions invaded Helvetia in the first century A.D., they were accompanied by mastiffs, whose descendants were being used to protect the flocks in the Alpine cantons in southwest Switzerland. In the eighteenth century, the monks in hospices on the Saint Bernard pass noticed its extraordinary sense of direction on mountains and its protective instincts, and decided to use it to help travellers in distress. Ginger and white with a black mask, this powerful breed, with a noble air and character, is divided into two varieties—longhaired and shorthaired. It stands about 28 inches tall and has a large powerful head and slightly rheumy eyes. It is good-natured. Right: Young Thom gazes with admiration at Dorf de Fontbuis de la Chenaie, owned by Mrs. Brault.

HOVAWART

Following double page: The protective attitude of Calik von Muniberg toward Mrs. Catherine Daniel illustrates the instinct of this dog, which was used by medieval peasants to protect their property. Rather tall, it can measure up to 28 inches and weigh about 90 pounds. Its coat, consisting of long, slightly wavy hair, can be blond, black or a black saddle with blond markings. This particularly useful dog is an excellent long-distance runner, capable of jumping over high and wide obstacles. Its bark is especially powerful.

ANATOLIAN SHEPHERD

In ancient times, this dog was used to protect flocks of sheep on the Anatolian plateau, bordered to the north by the Pontic Mountains, and to the south by the Taurus Mountains. Standing from 30 to 32 inches tall, with a powerful frame, it can accelerate extremely quickly. Its characteristic features are its broad powerful head, thick muscular neck, solid legs and curved upper line. Its fur can be short or medium and any colour, but is always dense. It tolerates all kinds of weather and is accustomed to living outdoors year round. Ardent and dynamic, it is also extraordinarily patient with children, like A'Palah with the children of Mr. and Mrs. Cerda.

Originally, this dog was just a variety of Newfoundland. When the English animal painter Landseer (1802-1873) was commissioned to paint a member of the British Lifesaver's Society, he chose to depict him with a black and white Newfoundland, the better to set off his subject. The picture was a great success and made this variety of Newfoundland so popular that British dog-lovers made it into a separate breed—which is pure morphological heresy—and naturally named it after the painter that had made it so popular. Later, the British lost interest, and continental European breeders were left to continue, hence the subtitle "continental-European type". This harmoniously shaped dog, as can be seen with Ulof Lonstrup du Kouif standing below Mr. and Mrs. Breton, has remained similar to the Newfoundland and shares its life-saving instinct. The difference is in its extremely long, smooth, dense fur, mixed with a lower layer that is thinner than the Newfoundland's. This fur gives it a white coat with discontinuous black patches.

PYRENEAN MASTIFF

Certain traits of this tall, powerful Spanish dog show its relation to France's Pyrenean mountain dog. This is not surprising, for the ancestor of both breeds was a primitive Asian mastiff.

With a maximum height of 32 inches, it has a broad skull and large solid head, topped by medium-sized drooping ears, which are flat and triangular. Its body is stout, its back powerful and its hindquarters wide and firm. Its strong thick tail has abundant tufts of fur. Its coat consists of dense thick fur and is generally white with grey or yellow patches, but it can also be brown, black, grey, beige or yellow.

This strong, courageous and quiet dog is also distinguished by extraordinary tenderness to its masters. Far right: Xoxona de la Tajadera del Tio Roy, belonging to Mr. Jean-François Trimolet, is fifteen months old.

PYRENEAN MOUNTAIN DOG

This breed arrived in the high valleys of the Ariège a long time ago. It was one of the Counts of Foix's favourite dogs. Its large size should eliminate the occasional confusions between it and the Pyrenean Shepherd. Measuring up to 32 inches tall, it has a powerful build. Its large snout narrows at the tip. Its chest is wide and deep, its back fairly long and its hindquarters oblique. Its flat abundant fur is supple and quite long, making for a magnificent coat that is generally plain white, with a few light yellow patches, or a uniform wolf-grey. It is easy to understand why its harmonious figure attracted television producers, who honoured it in the fine French television series devoted to Gaston Phébus, Comte de Foix, and made it the heroine of the series "Belle et Sébastien".

ABOVE: Delfin d'Elissacilio, Pyrenean Mountain Dog, owned by Mrs. Françoise Vidal.

GREAT SWISS MOUNTAIN DOG

This breed originated with the arrival in Switzerland of mastiffs with the Roman legions. This robust tricolour dog is the largest of the Swiss mountain and cattle dogs. Its head is topped with medium-sized ears that droop to the sides, and its body is powerful but not particularly large. It has a long straight back and a rather heavy tail. Its coat is black, with brilliant red and white symmetrical patches. This strong dog requires a firm but not brutal master. When well trained, it does its best to carry out the work its master gives it, and it listens to instructions with great concentration, just like Ebasile du Menhir des Mousseaux (far right), who never misses a single one of Mr. Forget's orders.

ENTLEBUCH CATTLE DOG

A probable descendant of Roman dogs, this small cattle dog—measuring a maximum of 20 inches—established itself in the mountains of Entlebuch, to the west of the Quatre-Cantons Lake, in Lucerne canton. Its small brown eyes are seductively vivacious. Its head is topped with drooping, medium-sized ears. It has a graceful body, and its tail is clipped at birth. The fur is short, dense, close to the body, wiry and brilliant. The coat is black with markings—over its eyes and on its cheeks and legs—that can range from yellow to rusty brown. It also has symmetrical white markings on its head, neck, chest and paws. Swiss cattle dogs are generally extremely mistrustful.

ABOVE: Benot, Entlebuch Cattle Dog, owned by Mr. Cecil Serfaty.

BERNESE MOUNTAIN DOG

The origins of this breed are controversial. However, all dog-lovers agree that its ancestors were good working dogs as early as the Middle Ages. The mountain folk of the high valleys in the canton of Berne generally used it to deliver their milk to the local cheese-maker in pails on a cart, which the Bernese mountain dog dragged along winding, bumpy paths. Fusain, Romain Paty's confidant, is a good example of this fairly large utilitarian dog (26 to 28 inches). The Bernese mountain dog has a powerful head, muscular neck, broad chest, straight back and rounded hindquarters. Its coat is black with reddish brown patches on its cheeks and legs. Its chest is white. Its fine fur is smooth, long and slightly wavy.

TERRIERS

G R O U P E 3

Dr. Fernand Méry was not only a great and popular animal lover, he was also an eminent cynologist who wrote numerous works concerning the origins and evolution of the canine species. He thus revealed the appearance in Egypt during the Middle Empire (2100 to 1850 B.C.) of a small, rather elongated dog that looked like a basset hound. Had it derived from an Egyptian greyhound? Fernand Méry remained silent on this point. He simply stated that he had discovered no earlier documents referring to this dog. Since the Phoenicians had already colonized the Syrian-Palestinian coastline in the second millennium B.C., and were thus neighbours of the Egyptians, it is possible that the descendants of this dog had evolved in

Phoenicia and that Phoenician sailors took some of them with them during their voyages to the British Isles. This hypothesis is accepted by numerous cynologists. Whatever the real story, it is certain that short-legged dogs, capable of pursuing badgers and foxes into their dens, thrived in the British Isles more than 2,000 years ago. And in fact, most of the modern breeds of terrier come from Britain. The creators of these breeds tried above all to obtain dogs that could hunt foxes, badgers, martens and polecats underground, and destroy rodents. This is why these breeds are generally rather aggressive, dynamic and courageous. They also share many morphological characteristics, such as their small size, which enables them to crawl into burrows, and their powerful jaws.

With the arrival of modern methods of pest control, terriers have been used less and less to carry out their initial task. Only three breeds are officially still used (the Fox Terrier, the German Hunting Terrier and the Airedale, although the latter hunts only above ground). The other breeds are generally pets, and it is rare that their masters make them work.

At about 20 inches, this is the largest of the Irish terriers. Created in the nineteenth century, it probably resulted from a cross between various terriers from the county of Kerry. Its powerful head is crowned with thin ears near the front. The body is muscular and well developed. Its broad back is straight, and its thin tail is erect. Its smooth, abundant, wavy fur can be any shade of blue. Mr. and Mrs. Rochette rightly claim that if the Kerry Blue does use its strength to gain other dogs' respect, it can also be sociable. Hazel-Boy Grenemore (far right) is an excellent example of this trait.

This breed was obtained by crossing a Dandie Dinmont Terrier with a Whippet in Northumberland. The miners of the region appreciated its remarkable qualities as a ratter and, at the beginning of the nineteenth century, used it to destroy the rodents that plagued their mine shafts. Of average height, it measures about 16 inches. This is a gracious, supple and muscular dog. Its pear-shaped head, long neck and arched back make it look like a lamb, even more so given that its thick fur tends to curl. Its coat is blue, fawn or brown. The Bedlington is generally friendly and is constantly trying to prove its loyalty, yet it has still not lost its original vivacity and liveliness.

ABOVE: Wetop Juggler, Bedlington, owned by Mrs. Mallet.

LAKELAND TERRIER

This English terrier originated in the nineteenth century, in the Lake District below the southwest border of Scotland and near to the Irish Sea. Like the Border Terrier, which comes from the same region but to the east, its job was to kill the foxes that were decimating the flocks of sheep. Elegant, with a well proportioned head, its ears are V-shaped. Its back is short and strong, its tail docked and erect. Its maximum height is 15 inches, and its fur is dense and wiry. Its coat can be black and tan, blue and tan, red, blond, brown, blue or black. Like Patterdale Ivory in Mrs. Liselotte Accarie's arms (right), Lakeland terriers make perfect pets. But they still have not lost their hunting instincts.

BORDER TERRIER

This breed was created in Cumberland, in the extreme northwest region of England, on the Scottish border (hence its name). Developed for hunting foxes, it performed a great service to the sheep farmers of the region. Its characteristic otter-shaped head is topped with small V-shaped ears. Its body is quite long, but its tail fairly short. Its coarse dense fur forms a coat that can be red, pale fawn, grey and yellow, or brown. Able to keep pace with a horse, this dog was first bred to work but now generally lives as a pet. Some owners, however, go out of their way to make their dogs work, and so maintain the breed's qualities. Morgan, Mrs. Sandrine Charmeaux's young son, gets along with with S'Mady Lady, Denfert, Everly, Froosty, Malice, Garish Blue and Guatemala, who are his good friends (following double page).

AIREDALE TERRIER

Following double page: In comparison with Darling Rose from Sealyham House, who is a Sealyham Terrier, Eline des Korils d'Armor (who also belongs to Mr. Prin and Mr. Thual) shows us that the Airedale Terrier (25 inches) is the largest of all of the terriers. As its name suggests, it was created in the mid-nineteenth century in the valley of the River Aire, near Leeds in the north of England. There were many otters in this valley, and the local hunters wanted a specialized dog to capture them. With this in mind, they crossed an otterhound with an old British terrier that is now extinct. The Airedale's body is black and grey. Its head and ears are tan. Its slightly wavy fur is dense and wiry. The ears on its long head are V-shaped. Its back is short, strong and straight. Its docked tail is highly placed. As its size does not allow it to enter burrows, some hunters use it to hunt stags as well as otters. It is also an excellent defender.

SEALYHAM TERRIER

Like the Airedale Terrier, the ancestor of Mr. Prin's Darling Rose from Sealyham House (far right) was created to hunt otters, but underground in their burrows rather than in streams. The Sealyham was also developed during the second half of the nineteenth century on the banks of the Seal, a stream that crosses the village of Sealyham in the extreme southwestern point of Wales. No taller than 12 inches, it has fearsome square jaws. Its neck is thick and muscular, and its body of medium length. Its short back legs are strong. Its tail is straight. Its long wiry fur is either completely white, or white with lemon-yellow markings. Despite its remarkable hunting talents, it is now generally kept as a pet.

GERMAN HUNTING TERRIER

Like the German Shepherd, the creation of this species was due to the wave of nationalism that followed the declaration of the German Empire. In the early twentieth century, some German foresters decided to create a terrier capable of replacing the British breeds. But, paradoxically, they were forced to use several British breeds of terrier to achieve their goal, especially the Fox Terrier and the Welsh Terrier. Of average height, it stands between 13 and 16 inches tall. It has a powerful snout, strong teeth and drooping V-shaped ears. Its limbs are muscular and its docked tail horizontal or slightly erect. Its wiry or smooth fur is generally black, but can also be a mixture of black and grey or brown with fawn markings. It is always an active explorer of burrows and can be a good game retriever. Right: Colt Pyram de la Jalletière, owned by Mr. Jacques Georget.

IRISH GLEN OF IMAAL TERRIER

Although rare, this Irish dog belongs
to one of the oldest breeds of terrier.
At 13 inches tall, its broad head is
decked with slightly rose-shaped ears.
It has a strong chest, an elongated body
and a docked tail. Its fur is of medium
length, coarse and either brindled blue
or blond. It was a formidable hunter,
but is now generally a pet, as can be
seen with Ivanhoe's Amadeus, pictured
here with the daughter of his owner,
Mr. Gerhard Knieling.

IRISH TERRIER

Some cynologists consider that this breed already existed in the eighteenth century. In fact, it does not seem to have been created until the late nineteenth century, using various local breeds. Its long head, with powerful jaws, is topped with small ears that droop down onto its cheeks. Its neck is long, its back extremely straight and its docked tail highly placed. Its wiry fur gives it a uniform red coat. Fiery, impetuous and courageous, it has a good nature and, when at rest, it looks as calm as Joe von der Leimkaul (right), pictured here pressing himself against Jean-Paul Péresse. Joe's sociability does not stop him from showing his courage when necessary. After ousting eight boars from their wallow with his companion, he confronted a 360-pound sow to save a wounded dog.

FOX TERRIER

Between the fifteenth and eighteenth centuries, many authors wrote of the exploits of the Fox Terrier. These accounts refer to two English breeds that are now extinct, the Black and Tan Terrier, and the White Terrier. The modern Fox Terrier came into being in the nineteenth century from a cross between these two breeds, first the smooth variety, then, a few years later, the wire-haired variety. The latter has become famous thanks to Hergé's comic books about the adventures of Tintin and his wire-haired terrier, Milou. The Fox Terrier has extremely powerful jaws, small V-shaped ears that droop down over its cheeks, a short straight back and a highly placed docked tail. Its coat is white with brown and black patches. Both varieties display great vivacity and speed. The Fox Terrier still has an inclination to dig out prey, and its strength makes it an excellent retriever of small game.

Fox Terrier (smooth)

This dog's fur is smooth, straight, flat, and dense. Smooth Touch At Travella is extremely sharp and alert. Highly sociable, he is happy only when he is with Mr. Patrice Legros (right), who in turn knows that he can rely on him.

Fox Terrier (wire)

This terrier's wiry fur is extremely stiff, never woolly or silky, thick or shaggy. All Fox Terriers are headstrong and brave, but also rather stubborn. Therefore they need a master who can control them and give them space and time to work off their energy every day. If this is the case, this dog will give its master wonderful friendship and loyalty.

BLACK RUSSIAN TERRIER

This breed was created after World War II according to instructions from Soviet authorities who wanted to provide their kolkhozes with dogs that could herd and defend flocks, as well as hunt. Loyd Antoshka, standing above Mrs. Brigitte Monfort, shows the anomaly in classifying this large dog, which is 28 inches high, among the terriers. This comes from the fact that this breed has been recognized only very recently by the World Canine Organisation which took the easy way out by classifying it according to its name. But it would be more logical to place it in the second group, for the Giant Schnauzer was almost certainly one of the breeds used to create it. Strong and powerful, it has a long head with whiskers and a small beard, a high broad chest and a thick docked tail. Its coarse, wiry, abundant fur is extremely dense and forms a black coat that can contain grey hairs. Rustic and robust, it can adapt to any weather conditions.

PARSON JACK RUSSELL TERRIER

In the early nineteenth century, Jack Russell decided to create a breed of terrier corresponding to his hunting ideas. Unfortunately, after his death, the examples produced veered from the original type, and it was only in the 1970s that breeders returned to the model created by Parson Russell. This is why this breed is now only provisionally recognized by the World Canine Organisation. Standing at 12 inches, with a finely balanced head, strong straight back and extremely solid legs, this terrier is an active and swift dog, full of stamina and bred to work. Its thick coat is made up of coarse dense fur which can be either smooth or wiry. It is white and can contain fawn, lemon-yellow or black markings. Right: Gipsy du Pré Mil, owned by Mr. Bernard Lelyon.

AUSTRALIAN TERRIER

When the first British settlers went to Australia, they took their dogs with them. The Australian terrier is the result of crosses made between various breeds of terrier that had thus been imported, particularly the Cairn terrier, the Dandie Dinmont, the Skye terrier and the Yorkshire terrier. The breed became firmly established at the end of the nineteenth century. Standing 10 inches tall, it is low and compact. It has a long head, with small pointed ears, a rather long body, a straight back and a docked tail. Its straight fur is of a wiry texture and gives it a blue or silver-grey coat, with tan patches on the legs and snout. It has kept its ability to hunt, but when necessary it can stay as calm.

ABOVE: Dare Devils Magic Mirabunda, Australian Terrier, owned by Mrs. Bonne Pracomtal.

CAIRN TERRIER

Authors referred to this breed as early as the eighteenth century. Its name comes from its ability to hunt: the mounds of rock and earth in which foxes and badgers often take shelter are called "cairns" in Scotland. In honour of this dog's determination and skill in finding a way through the brambles covering these mounds in pursuit of prey, the Scots called it the "cairn". Weighing 13 pounds and standing 12 inches tall, this alert dog has a small head topped with pointed ears, a straight back and a short highly placed tail. It has a solid bone structure stands firmly upright. It has abundant and wiry, but not shaggy, fur. Its coat can be sandy, grey, dark grey or pepper and salt. The Cairn Terrier requires almost no upkeep. This small, active, cheerful terrier can be a little stubborn, but as it always want to please its masters, it can overcome its own petulance. Preceding double page: Djinn Fizz, Feeling, Etna et Élysée (all four "de la Terrardière") with Yann Fontaine.

WELSH TERRIER

French dog experts affirm that the Welsh terrier descends from a terrier that lived with the Celts and took refuge with them in the mountains of Wales during the Roman invasion. For many centuries, it was used to hunt vermin, foxes, badgers and otters. It has thus become a great worker. With a maximum height of 16 inches, it is slightly smaller than its ancestors. Its square build gives it a distinguished air. Its flat skull widens slightly between small V-shaped ears. Its back is short, its legs solid and its docked tail highly placed. Its wiry fur is extremely dense and abundant, giving it a black and tan or greyish black and tan coat, with its head and legs. An excellent working dog, full of vivacity, it can also be a great pet, as Athos des Chardons Saint-André (right) is for Mrs. Reiter.

CESKY TERRIER

This is the most recent breed of terrier. By recognizing it ten years ago, the World Canine Organisation honoured the serious work of its creator, Mr Horak, an enthusiastic fox hunter who wanted a dog especially suited to the conditions in Bohemia. To achieve his goal, he crossed Scottish Terriers with Sealyham Terriers. The Cesky Terrier stands a maximum of 14 inches tall. It is a rather low dog, with a long head, powerful neck and medium-length body. Its shaggy fur gleams like silk. Light and agile, it is perfectly suited to the work it was designed for. The two terriers sitting on either side of Alexandra Benech (right) belong to Mrs. Delplanque. They display the colours of their breed: blue grey (Landru de Schalckes) and brown (Dolly de la Fontaine de Villiers).

DANDIE DINMONT TERRIER

In the eighteenth century, terriers were extremely popular in Scotland. Gypsies started meeting each year to compare the qualities of their terriers in a long work trial, after which they crossed the best dogs. The Dandie Dinmont emerged from crossings between the best terriers. This breed became famous when one of Walter Scott's characters had a pack of them. The novel in question was an enormous success, and the name of the character, Dandie Dinmont, was given to the breed. It is small but has a powerful head. Its long, low body is strong and supple, rather like a weasel. Its has extremely muscular short legs, a low, arched, back and a tail that curves like a scimitar. Its fur is wiry and coarse, the coat fawn or pepper ranging from blackish to blue or light grey). Left to right in front of Mr. Stéphane Segal: Babeloona du Nid des Flibustiers, who belongs to Mr. Segal, and German's Dandie Beauty Barina, Gwennie and Ghillie de la Valoise de Bréançon, who belong to Mrs. Tessier.

NORWICH TERRIER

This small terrier, which must be a maximum of 10 inches tall, was created in the late nineteenth century when a local tan-coloured terrier (many varieties exist between Cambridge and Norwich), was crossed with Bedlingtons, Bull Terriers and Irish Terriers. Initially, there were two varieties: one with erect ears and one with drooping ears. Created by Mr Jones, they finally developed into two different breeds. The Norwich Terrier is solid, low and has a horizontal tail. Its snout is powerful and shaped rather like a wedge, and the medium-sized pointed ears must be erect—illustrated perfectly by Scarlet Runners Harlekin (far right), nestled in Mrs. Bonne de Pracomtal's arms. The fur is wiry, straight and lies flat against the body. The coat is red, blond, black and tan or greyish.

NORFOLK TERRIER

The only distinguishing characteristic of the Norfolk Terrier is its ears. They are medium-sized, V-shaped, slightly rounded at the tip and droop forward over the cheeks. This essential difference is clearly visible in Miss Ardina Strüwer's Easy That's Me (below), nicknamed Busy. Originally, the Norfolk and Norwich Terriers were otters and rabbits hunters. Although they are now generally household pets, they have retained their athletic abilities and, despite their short legs, are rapid runners.

ABOVE: Easy That's me, Norfolk Terrier, owned by Ardina Strüwer.

WEST HIGHLAND WHITE TERRIER

This breed owes its elegance to a mistake made by Colonel de Poltaloch. This great huntsman used to track foxes and rabbits with small fawn-colored Highland Terriers. One day, thinking that he was firing at a fox hidden in the undergrowth, he killed one of his own dogs. He immediately decided that from that day forward he would have only white dogs and, after careful selections, managed to fix the West Highland White, known now to its many enthusiasts as the "Westie". It is often used in advertizing, which is understandable given its attractive appearance, elegance and mischievous looks, as in this group that consists of French Lover de Champernoune, Call Me the Champ de Champernoune and Excentricity de Champernoune with Mrs. Amato and Mrs. Round-Vanlaer. The Westie is compact and energetic. Its small, straight ears top its mischievous face. Its back is straight, its tail is short and erect and its straight, wiry fur is white.

SCOTTISH TERRIER

Scottish Terriers, which descend from the Celts' Terriers, have developed into different breeds according to regional selection criteria. In the northwest Highlands, they are squat with wiry fur. In the Western Isles, they have elongated bodies and long fur. In the east, they have short legs and large heads. The Scottish terrier is, in some respects, a synthesis of various breeds of eastern terriers. Its squat, powerful figure is well known to whisky lovers, as it can be seen on the label of a famous brand. It has a long head, topped with straight pointed ears, a muscular neck, a rather short back and a medium-length tail that can be erect or slightly curved. Its fur is dense, wiry and coarse and forms a blond or brindled coat. Although the Scottish terrier is no longer used as a working dog, it has still kept its ancestors' agility and energy. Right: Émeraude des Rives du Morbras, owned by Mrs. Delplanque.

BULL TERRIER

This breed was created in about 1860 by Mr Hinks, a British dog-lover who always refused to reveal the breeds he had used. He is believed to have used the bulldog and the British White Terrier with, perhaps, the Greyhound and the Pointer. The breed was fixed at the end of the nineteenth century. It became popular again with the American television series, "Hogan's Heroes", about the adventures of a fighter squadron that had a bull terrier as its mascot. There are two categories of this breed.

MINIATURE

This dog differs from the standard only in that its height is limited to 13 inches.

STANDARD

This dog is characterized by its long, oval head, topped by small, slim straight ears. Its back is short and straight and its short horizontal tail is low. Its fur is flat, short and harsh to the touch, creating a coat that can be pure white or black, red, fawn or tricoloured, providing white is the dominant colour.

Neither its height nor its weight is limited. What is important is that the dog be well proportioned. First Sitting Bull du Mockcastel's behaviour surprises Mr. Michel Gauvrit each evening: he slips into the living room, collects the cushions from the armchairs and carefully takes them to the corner of the house where he sleeps, making a comfortable bed for himself.

ABOVE: Bull Terrier, owned by Miss Fety.

AUSTRALIAN SILKY TERRIER

This breed was created in the late nineteenth century by Australian breeders who crossed Australian terriers with Yorkshires. Standing 9 inches tall, this dogs is compact and fairly long. It has small, round and lively eyes. Its head is topped with small V-shaped ears, which are thin, high and erect. Its back is straight and the docked tail is horizontal, but not erect. Its fine beautiful coat is composed of extremely silky, shiny hair, which is about six inches long. It is blue and tan or blue-grey and tan. This breed still has the terriers' characteristic instincts and, whenever it discovers a rat, it immediately kills it.

ENGLISH TOY TERRIER (BLACK AND TAN)

This is, in fact, a version of a Manchester Terrier, obtained by selecting the smallest dogs of that breed, and continuing the process until the desired size had been reached. As Mr. Guy Gland demonstrates, Brynlythe Florine (right) is small enough to be taken anywhere, especially as these toy terriers, which weigh about 7 pounds, can be extremely discreet. This does not stop them from being brave and energetic the rest of the time. The English Toy Terrier (Black and Tan) is compact, but its pure lines give it an indisputable elegance. Its short, gleaming fur needs no upkeep.

ABOVE: Casa de Casey Sassy de Satsy, Silky Terrier, owned by Mr. François Istas.

AMERICAN STAFFORDSHIRE TERRIER

This American breed is the result of crosses between the Bull Terrier and the Staffordshire Bull Terrier, established in England. With its high, medium-length head topped with short erect ears, high broad chest, muscular body, short slightly sloped back and short tail, it gives an impression of great power. It stands about 19 inches tall. Its fur is short, dense and harsh to the touch and shiny. Activity is essential to this energetic, dynamic breed. It can be an excellent guard dog when correctly trained, but its master must use firm discipline. Preceding double page: Hagele's Hotshot, nicknamed Charly (owned by Mr. Frédéric Chauvineau), is pictured with Miss Berruet, who regrets the fact that some people in the United States train the American Staffordshire to make it dangerous. This is a disservice to the dog, as the media perpetuates negative generalizations about this breed.

STAFFORDSHIRE BULL TERRIER

The dog was created by crossing the old Bull Terrier breed with various other British terriers in Staffordshire. This terrier became extremely popular in Britain after World War II. Measuring between 14 and 16 inches tall, it is well-proportioned and very muscular. Its head, topped with roseate, half-erect ears, is short and high. Its neck is short, body stocky and legs solid. Its coat is red, fawn, black, blue, variegated white or pure white. The fur is smooth, short and thick. Intrepid and brave, it needs a firm but kind master. This lively dog will then be as calm and affectionate as Fox Lady de la Lune de Sang and Funny Droopy de la Lune de Sang, pictured with Mr. and Mrs. Petit (right).

YORKSHIRE TERRIER

This breed was created in the county of Yorkshire, in northern England, supposedly by poachers, who wanted to conduct their illegal activities using a small terrier. Most breeders believe that they achieved this goal by crossing Cairn Terriers with the Maltese Bichon, which accounts for the dog's marvellous coat. The breed was officially registered in 1886. At under 7 pounds, this dog has a compact build. Its small, rather flat head is topped with small, erect V-shaped ears. Its back is straight, and its closely docked tail rises up high. Its beautiful, long, silky coat is dark steel-blue on the body, and fawn on the head and lower legs. Despite their appearance, the "Yorkie" (as it is called by its fans) is robust and athletic. But this joyful, lively and intelligent charmer also makes a perfect pet. Right: Djebel Amour, French Cancan, Gueule de Loup and Gage d'Amour, owned by Miss Pascale Mark.

SKYE TERRIER

Originally from the Isle of Skye, in the Outer Hebrides, this breed combines the various qualities of the Hebridean terriers. Its long, low body and abundant fur give it its characteristic appearance. This dog became popular with several generations of children when it appeared as the puppet Dougal in the "Magic Roundabout" television show. Its long, powerful head is topped with ears that are generally erect. Its long, flat, wiry fur never curls. It forms a coat that can be light or dark grey, black, fawn or cream. Perhaps because of this marvellous coat, dog lovers generally keep them as pets, rather than as hunters, which they once were.

DACHSHUNDS

The fourth group is unique in that it contains just one breed. This classification was the subject of long debates in the World Canine Organisation, as several countries objected to the idea of one breed constituting an entire group. But Germany, the breed's country of origin and thus its technical director, demonstrated that the Dachshund's physical characteristics and skills make it a separate breed. Although the World Canine Organisation was not entirely convinced by Germany's morphological arguments, it did agree that this formidable working dog performs highly diverse tasks: it hunts foxes and badgers in burrows, like the terriers that form the third group, and it hunts above ground by "voice tracking", in other words, the dachshund barks and follows a rabbit's or hare's trail as do scent hounds in the sixth group. Furthermore, the Dachshund often works in packs like scent hounds. It can follow large, wounded prey by tracking its blood. For many years, this was the only dog to do so, but it has since been joined by various breeds in the seventh group (Pointers). These arguments were sufficient to convince the World Canine Organisation. The exact origin of this German basset is still a controversial subject among cynologists. Some believe that it came from Egypt, but supporters of this hypothesis have not explained how it travelled from Egypt to Germany. Others think that it descended from German brachets—scent hounds—in the Middle Ages. This hypothesis seems the most plausible. The Dachshund has flat, medium-length, rounded ears. They are placed high and behind its long head. Its lean, muscular neck is quite long. Its body is long and compact. Intelligent and lively, it barks only when necessary. When this working dog has a firm but fair master, it is an excellent companion. There are three categories of Dachshunds, distinguished by their fur: short, wiry and long. Each category is subdivided into three sizes. The Standard Dachshund weighs a maximum of 20 pounds, the ideal weight being between 14 to 16 pounds. The Miniature Dachshund must weigh under nine pounds at eighteen months and the chest measurement may not exceed 14 inches. The Rabbit (or Rabbit-hunting) Dachshund may not weigh more than 8 pounds at eighteen months, and the chest may not exceed 12 inches.

SMOOTH-HAIRED DACHSHUND

Short, thick, shiny flat fur covers its entire body.

STANDARD SMOOTH-HAIRED DACHSHUND

Right: Fleurine de Mostavielle, leaning on Mr. Serge Mallet's shoulder, illustrates two of the Dachshund's traits: sociability and liveliness.

MINIATURE SMOOTH-HAIRED DACHSHUND

Following double page: Next to Bout'chou de la Voûte Azurée, a Standard Dachshund (to the right), Mrs. Jeannine Chopin presents a fine set of Miniature Smooth-Haired Dachshunds, in particular Douce and Patchouli de Sadiana.

LONG-HAIRED DACHSCHUND

This dog's fur is silky, soft, flat and slightly curly. Below: owned by Mrs. Gérard Goguelat.

MINIATURE LONG-HAIRED DACHSCHUND

Félicihossy and Élodie Jacops (right).

LONG-HAIRED RABBIT DACHSCHUND

Frissondamour du Dom Teckel (left).

WIRE-HAIRED DACHSHUND

This dog's fur is the same length all over the body and forms a dense, wiry coat.

MINIATURE WIRE-HAIRED DACHSHUND

Cyrano du Creux de la Sablière (above) and with M. Ernest Roussel-Lagache (right).

WIRE-HAIRED RABBIT DACHSHUND

MINIATURE SMOOTH-HAIRED DACHSHUND

Fergusalbert de l'Ancien Relais, a black and tan Miniature Dachshund, with Mr. Jean Wattement.

GROUPE 5

This group includes the breeds that have remained the closest to the animal from which the canine species evolved. They have kept certain characteristics: erect ears, wedge-shaped faces, a tail rolled up over the back or hindquarters. Some breeds share all these characteristics. These are of the "primitive type". Other breeds have different transmittable characteristics, complementary to the ones just cited: small triangular ears, abundant fur with a thick undercoat. These belong to the "Spitz type," which includes the Nordic breeds (dogs from the Artic), European Spitzes, Asian Spitzes and related breeds. The many Arctic breeds are divided according to the work they do: huskies, hunting dogs, guard dogs and sheepdogs (for protecting and leading flocks). This group also contains breeds that used to be classified with the sight hounds. They originate from the Mediterranean basin, hunt rabbits and have two of the primitive dog's important characteristics: erect ears and a wedge-shaped head. The development of vehicles designed specifically for the Arctic has led to a progressive drop in the use of sled dogs as a means of transport. Concerned with maintaining these dogs' particular abilities, cynophiles have set up work trials and use the results to determine which dogs will be the best reproducers. A love of competition has led some people to organize sled contests—quite unrelated to the work trials—that have been rather successful. The desire to win at all costs has pushed some competitors into experimenting with hazardous crosses in the hope of obtaining faster dogs. Because of this abuse, France's Central Canine Society warned the World Canine Organisation that it should not tolerate such practices and that new breeds can be created, with all the necessary precautions, only if none of the four hundred officially registered breeds is capable of carrying out a given specific task useful to mankind in general.

SIBERIAN HUSKY

This breed originally comes from northeast Siberia, where the Chukchi nomads have always used it to draw their sleds and hunt. Contrary to a widely held view, huskies do not necessarily have blue eyes. They can be brown, and they can even have one blue eye and one brown eye. Its snout is of medium length, its triangular ears are placed high on the head, its chest is high and strong, its average-length back is straight and solid, and its great poise makes it look extremely elegant. Its double-layered fur is of medium length, and its coat can be any colour from white to black. Of average height—between 21 and 24 inches—it is above all a working dog that carries out its job extremely efficiently, pulling light loads at moderate speed over great distances. It is not adapted to city life and tends to run away from home.

GREENLAND DOG

Originally from Greenland, this dog is full of strength and stamina and is used to working in the harshest conditions of the Arctic. It has successfully participated in numerous expeditions to both the North and South poles. Despite its tendency to run away from home, the Greenland Dog is sociable. However, it is exceptional for it to be as affectionate to its master as Amaraqs D'Giro is to Mr. Delente, for it is not naturally demonstrative. It stands at least 24 inches, has a strong neck, very broad chest, an extremely muscular body and a straight back. Its coat is made up of dense, straight, coarse fur, and can be any colour. Kept outside constantly by the Greenlanders, it has become strong and can easily withstand both cold and heat. It is now used as a sled dog only by the Eskimos and by Arctic hunters.

ABOVE: Amaraqs D'Giro, Greenland Dog, owned by Mr. Delente.

ALASKAN MALAMUTE

Attachment to its masters is one of the characteristics of this large powerful dog, originally from the Bay of Kotzbuhe on the Bering Straits. Its name comes from the Eskimo tribe to which it provided indispensable help for centuries. It is the largest of the sled dogs. With its deep compact chest and vigorous and powerful build, it carries out its work efficiently, pulling heavy loads over great distances. Its eyes are brown, preferably dark brown, and never blue. Its thick, coarse coat has two color combinations (grey and brown, or black and white) or else is pure white. It adapts well to bad weather conditions but dislikes great heat. Full of dignity, calm and determination, Umalooil Over Vale and Dale is inseparable from his mate, Arctic Black Gipsy Over Vale and Dale (right), who, under Mrs. Raust de Palma's direction, participates with him in the work trials organized by the French Nordic dog club.

SAMOYED

This large dog—an average 23 inches—takes its name from the Samoyeds, a tribe in northern Siberia. It kept their herds, hunted bears with them and pulled their sleds. Its ample, heavy, dense and supple fur forms a coat that can be white, or sandy and white. This energetic dog is robust and agile. Full of dignity, it makes an excellent pet that attaches itself to its masters, as can be seen with Mrs. Arlette Flamand when she talks of her relationship with Blue Sky's Dapper Dan and Ivory Madonna of Sameida (following double page).

NORWEGIAN ELKHOUND GREY

Standing at 21 inches, with an ample chest, a short and relatively compact body, this dog has a thick coat which is coarse and weather resistant and made up of long grey hair that is darker at its tips. Originally from Norway, it has always been considered a great hunter. Full of power, stamina and courage, it has a good nose and, for the Vikings, it provided exceptional help in the difficult task of tracking elk. In 1991, the Central Canine Society finally accepted that its scent abilities could be evaluated in tests involving tracking the blood of large wounded game. The Forestry and Water Resource Commission are planning to use it to record populations of game animals in order to better protect them.

Despite its great sociability, the Norwegian Elkhound is very independent.

FINNISH SPITZ

The ancestors of this breed were the companions of Finland's first inhabitants. When looking at Finn' Fellow de la Cascade des Jarreaux in front of Mr. Robeaux, one might think that the Finnish Spitz is a large dog, but this is an optical illusion caused by the camera angle. It is actually average in height—between 18 and 20 inches. Its body is almost square with a strong straight back. Its eyes, ear movements and wagging tail reveal its great vivacity and enthusiasm. Its short fur, lying close to its body, forms a ginger-brown or ginger-yellow coat. In Finland it is used for grouse hunting.

ABOVE: Djerva du Rocher de Sisyphe, Norwegian Elkhound Grey, owned by Mr. and Mrs. Christian Collas.

NORWEGIAN LUNDEHUND

This breed originally came from the Lofoten and Vesterälen Islands in the Atlantic, on the northwest coast of Norway. On the cliffs of these islands can be found many puffins, which the inhabitants of the archipelago capture live using these dogs. It climbs up the steepest cliffs with remarkable agility, for each of its feet is equipped with six claws, an exception in the canine species. Its coat, composed of rich dense fur, is ginger-brown, black or grey with white markings. It is light and generally jovial and perky. Its extraordinary suppleness allows it to throw back its head onto its back. It then contracts the cartilage around its ears to make them watertight. These two characteristics allow it to work in narrow damp caves.

KARELIAN BEAR DOG

Karelia straddles the Russo-Finnish border. This extremely ancient breed comes from the Russian part of the region. After the 1917 Revolution, the Russians lost interest in this dog, and the Finns adopted it. It is of average height — 22 to 24 inches — robust, strong and slightly longer than it is tall. It has a thick coat made up of stiff straight fur. It is black, preferably brownish or matte, with white markings or patches on its neck, chest, abdomen and legs. Its sense of smell is highly developed, which makes it of great help when hunting big game, as do its perseverance and courage. According to popular belief— which unfortunately is inaccurate—this dog supposedly has a difficult character. Björnehusets Gordon and Björnehusets Gaia (right) always obey young Chloé Meyer and are loving, loyal dogs.

ABOVE: Norwegian Lundehund, owned by Mrs. Robert.

SWEDISH VALLHUND

This small dog—13 inches—has adapted well to France, where the breed's first subject was imported by Mrs. Jocelyne Thomas in 1988. It is an extremely ancient Swedish breed. The Vikings entrusted it with their herds and houses and took it with them in their longboats on their expeditions, particularly to the British Isles. This was how several of these dogs first arrived in Wales, where they mated with local dogs, creating the Welsh Corgi, which greatly resembles it physically. Low to the ground, its elongated body is muscular and its neck long. Its wiry half-length fur forms a grey coat, with darker hairs on the back, the nape of the neck, shoulders and sides. It is a herd leader that can dominate any kind of cattle. Essentially a rural dog, it can adapt to city life.

ICELAND SHEEPDOG

It is only natural that young Margot Lembrez be extremely proud to hold G'Käta in her arms, for it is the first Iceland Sheepdog to be imported into France, thanks to Mrs. Jocelyne Thomas. G'Käta belongs to a breed that has existed for one thousand years. In the tenth century, Iceland became home to a large number of Norwegian and Swedish immigrants. The immigrants' dogs naturally mated with the indigenous primitive spitzes, which are now extinct. The Iceland sheepdog derives from this melting pot. Its coat consists of white wiry fur with fawn markings and black spots. This light, lively dog is an excellent flock leader. It can also be used as a guard dog. Made for living in the countryside, it becomes very attached to its masters and loves playing with children.

ABOVE: Drammerican's Biba, Swedish Vallhund, owned by Miss Edwige Thomas.

FINNISH REINDEER HERDER

Mrs. Catherine Agnus—seen here with her dogs Lumiturpa Baksu Bake (twenty months) and Katrin Onerva (four months), and Finntrix Tupu (three years) who belongs to Mr. Trichet— loves running by the sea with her four Nordic dogs. After taking part in the Nantes dog show, she took them to Saint-Brévin beach where they were so excited that they all fell into a deep pool of water. She was then able to see just how well they can swim. The Finnish Reindeer Herder is a dog of average height—maximum 21 inches—slightly longer than it is tall. Its long thick coat is composed of stiff fur, which can be of any colour. The first settlers in Iceland used it to guard their herds of reindeer. Very resistant, brave and easy to train, this rural dog makes an excellent sheepdog. It is also intelligent and calm, and is now generally kept as a pet.

GERMAN SPITZ

The ancestors of this dog lived with the first inhabitants of the lakeside towns. It fulfilled many roles: hunting, protection, sledding and companionship. Originally, the Spitz was a large dog, but its morphology has evolved during the centuries, at first naturally, and over the last two centuries through selective breeding. There are five varieties of modern spitz, essentially distinguished by their size. All have superb, abundant fur whose hair stands up above a dense underlayer. Their neck is covered with a large collar that forms a mane. Their fox-like head, bright intelligent eyes and the great mobility of their ears makes them look alert, curious and a little mischievous. Their mistrust of strangers, faithfulness to their masters and attachment to their home adds to their excellent qualities as companions.

Below: Miniature Spitz, Elton du Bois de Moque Souris, owned by Mrs. Monique Bourgalay.

POMERANIAN

This dog measures between 9 and 11 inches. Its coat can be wolf-grey like Cassius du Val de l'Ange Blanc or orange like Voyou du Val de l'Ange Blanc, owned by Mrs. Jacqueline Desouche (right). But it can also be black or white.

MINIATURE SPITZ

This dog measures from 8 to 11 inches tall. Its coat can be orange, white, brown, black or wolf-grey (see preceding page).

MEDIUM SPITZ

This dog measures from 12 to 14 inches. Its coat can be white, like Mrs. Jacqueline Peracini's Elphy du Périgord Vert, or black, brown, orange or wolf-grey. Queen Victoria had several of them, and enjoyed playing with them as relaxation from her heavy official duties.

GIANT SPITZ

Standing between 16 and 20 inches, its coat can be black, brown or white,

Below: Medium Spitz, owned by Mrs. Véronique Le Bihan and Mr. Éric Fongarnan.

KEESHOND

This is the largest of the spitzes. On average it stands 20 inches tall. Fendy zum Asphof and Igmar vom Osterhof display the beauty of their black-speckled sandy coat. Their paws, thighs and tails are light and the rest of the coat is charcoal grey with light markings over the shoulders. Along with Fendy and Igmar, Mr. Benoît Wiart has five other Keeshonds. After the birth of his daughter, the seven spitzes took turns going to the baby's bedroom, where they stood vigilantly on guard in front of her crib.

HOKKAIDO

Mr. Takumi Ashibe, who lives in Paris, appreciates the presence of Kumatorow Kouri and Katsume Tomikawa Toyada, his two Hokkaidos. Faithful, obedient and affectionate, they contribute to the Japanese atmosphere in his home. The Hokkaido lived with the Ainous in the Sakhalin, Kuril and Hokkaido islands to the north of Japan. In the eighth century, the Fujara clan seized power and pushed the Ainous back onto Hokkaido Island; this isolation helped conserve the purity of their dogs, which were generally used for bear hunting. It is now a guard dog. The Hokkaido, when in action, is swift, light and flexible. Of average height— 21 inches—and solidly built, it is well balanced. Its coat, composed of coarse straight fur, is black, ginger, brown or brindled. White is not appreciated, as the dog cannot be seen against the snow.

This large well-built dog is both stocky and well-proportioned. Originally from the province of Akita in Japan, it was the favourite companion of eighteenth-century Japanese nobles. In the nineteenth century, it was used in dog fights, before being replaced by the Tosa, a Molossian, and experiencing a rapid decline. After World War II, the Akita became popular once again. It is now Japan's national guard dog. Standing 27 inches tall, it has a harmonious build. Its coat, composed of coarse straight fur, is ginger, white or brindled. Mr. Patrick Suard first encountered an Akita in 1979. He was sleeping on Chiba beach, near Tokyo on the Pacific coast, when he was awoken by a large dog which, though sitting on its hind legs, was staring at him and barking. Attracted by its bear-like head, slanting eyes and powerful, yet elegant build, he obtained some information about the breed and purchased his first Akita. He has now been passionate about this breed for thirteen years, has started breeding them himself and praises their intelligence, docility, courage and nobility. It must be said that Daigoroh and Kasuga, standing on the podium, and Waka Obakosow and Hinaude Obakosow, in Mr. Suard's arms, justify his enthusiasm.

JAPANESE SPITZ

Even though, like all spitzes, its distant ancestor was the dog of the peat bogs, this is a relatively recent breed, the result of crosses between European and Japanese spitzes at the beginning of the twentieth century. It is a small well-shaped dog—measuring about 12 inches—and well proportioned. Its coat, made up of straight, erect fur, is abundant and pure white. Its snout is pointed, its ears triangular and erect. It carries its bushy tail over its back. The Japanese spitz is joyful, alert and brave. There are a few rare specimens in Europe, but none in France. Attracted by the international reputation of the Central Canine Society's annual dog show, Signora Luisella Gecchinato came from Italy to display Midori, who received much attention and praise.

EURASIER

Diva du Font du Roy, Phébus de Parayraou and Freya de Parayraou are three of Mrs. Mattei's eight Eurasiers (following double page). This recent breed was created in the 1950s from crosses between the Wolfspitz and the Chow Chow. Of average height—21 to 24 inches—it is compact and well-built, with a coat composed of both short dense fur and medium-length fur. It is black, grey-black or fawn. Calm and open, it adapts to any living conditions and is notably faithful. It is vigilant but not noisy, and barks only when necessary.

SHIBA

Originally from Hokurika, on the east coast of the island of Honshu to the northeast of Tokyo, this dog was previously used to hunt small game. It is now generally a pet. It is a short dog—16 inches—but nevertheless well-proportioned and muscular, like Welshim Osanu at Vormund in Mrs. Catherine Le Palec's arms. Its fur is coarse and straight. Its coat is black, black and tan, red, white or brindled. This lively, loyal and docile dog is both active and rapid. Like all of the "spitz type" dogs, it is extremely clean.

IBIZAN WARREN HOUND

Introduced into Spain by Phoenician sailors, the remarkable qualities of this rabbit hunter led the Spanish to introduce it to the Balearic Islands, where rabbits were causing considerable damage. The Ibizan Warren Hound is tall—up to 29 inches—and is a precocious hunter. Elodie (right) was only four months old when she caught her first rabbit. This attractive dog, with her red and white coat, is very attentive to the well-being of other animals. She took care of an unweaned kitten as well as she would have nurtured her own pup. She astonishes her owner Mr. Gilliot by the way she washes herself like a cat.

CHOW CHOW

The dog was the companion of the Huns, the Mongols and the Tartars, who used it as a guard dog and for hunting. English breeders became interested in this breed once relations were established between the West and China, after the Franco-British expedition of 1860. This is why the technical management of this Chinese breed is performed in Great Britain. The Chow Chow stands between 18 and 22 inches tall, is compact, powerful, imposing and has dense fur that can be long and brushed back, or short and straight. Its coat can be blue, like Oes-Ming-Chy-Nees, or a very light fawn like Arom-Pako, both of whom belong to Mr. Achille Lambert (right). It can also be whitish, or any shade of fawn. Its leonine appearance and grim expression, created by the wrinkles of the face, are characteristic. Other unusual aspects are its blue-black tongue and its short, stiff gait. It is dignified, calm and very attached to its masters despite an independent nature.

PHARAOH HOUND

This breed descends from a primitive African dog that accompanied Phoenician sailors during their expeditions. Some arrived in Malta, where they set up homes with their dogs. After taking possession of that island in 1800, the British became interested in the breed and christened it the "Pharaoh Hound," because of its similarity to a greyhound that appears frequently on ancient Egyptian monuments. The Pharaoh Hound is of average height and has a well-proportioned body. Its short, smooth, shiny fur gives it a fawn coat with white markings. It is a great rabbit hunter. Far right: Esaü Gaillard du Croquet, who belongs to Mrs. Françoise Gaillard and is pictured with Mr. Herman, illustrates this dog's noble poise, elegant carriage and erect ears. Its sense of hearing is extraordinary, and it hunts by ear as much as by sight.

CIRNECO DELL'ETNA

Like the Pharaoh Hound, the ancestor of this breed was the primitive African dog that accompanied Phoenician sailors. Some of these dogs settled in Sicily. It is of average height, generally about three inches shorter than the Pharaoh Hound. Its semi-smooth fur creates a "glassy" texture and gives a special appearance to its coat, which can be fawn and white or just fawn. This is a dynamic and extremely active breed and is both independent and very affectionate. Below: Faetano, owned by Mr. and Mrs. Henri Brelaud.

BASENJI

This dog's ancestors were already hunting with the Pygmies several thousands of years ago. It then became the companion of the Baschengi, a tribe based on the banks of the Congo in Western Africa. Later, the Egyptians considered it to be a sacred animal, responsible for leading the dead into the afterlife. There are two varieties of Basenji, both of which have short silky fur covering their baggy skin:
• the "brush" type, which measures a little over 16 inches and has a light fawn coat with a large white breastplate.
• the "wood" type, which is somewhat smaller and thus better suited to equatorial life. Its coat is dark fawn, almost mahogany.
In Africa, the Basenji works as a tracking dog for Safari guides, while villagers use it as a guard dog. It is ideally a rural dog, as it tends to run away from home. It is very clean and does not bark.

PORTUGUESE WARREN HOUND

The ancestor of this breed is a primitive African dog, introduced into the Canaries by the Phoenicians. It is an extremely muscular dog with great intelligence and extraordinary vivacity. There are three varieties: large, 22 to 28 inches; medium, 16 to 22 inches; and small, 8 to 12 inches. Elvira da Pria do Roberjo is the first dog of the small variety to be imported into France. The variety is so rare that Mrs. Jackie Bourdin had to wait two years before obtaining one. The fur is short, dense, smooth and fawn coloured, but the Portuguese Warren Hound's coat can also be long, coarse and coloured yellow, dark grey or faded black.

ABOVE: Edgiès Buckeye Traveler, Basenji, owned by Mr. Jean-Louis Grünheid.

SCENT HOUNDS
AND RELATED BREEDS

After this sixth canine category was formed, it was split into two subgroups: breeds used for hunting large game and other breeds used primarily for tracking wounded game. When assigning distinct breeds to the first group, the Canine Organisation based its decisions on the definition of a hound provided by Professor Triquet: "a hunting dog or hound with large, floppy ears that flushes out game thanks to a keen sense of smell and pursues it while continuously barking". A hound must therefore possess a strong constitution, keen sense of smell, powerful bark and an ability to pursue game tirelessly. The hound should also be sufficiently familiar with the game it is meant to pursue, well versed in its habits and tactics while it is being chased, and familiar with the natural terrain in which the game normally thrives. To accomplish all of that, the hound must be adequately trained and bred for the right characteristics, that is, it must be specialized in the pursuit of a particular type of game. Breeds that are specialized in the location of wounded game are assigned to the second group. This requires that the dog be able to pick up the wounded game's trail by detecting the blood spilled by the animal. The dog must be able to do this even when the trail has "gone cold", i.e., several hours after the animal has left the vicinity. Like other hunting dogs, bloodhounds must have a powerful bark, as this is the only means by which the hunter can follow the progress and direction of a high-speed chase through the countryside.

217

GREAT ANGLO-FRENCH TRICOLOUR HOUND

English and French hunting parties do not use their dogs in the same way. In England, the dogs are essentially trained to hunt in the open. In France, they are let loose on the trail, whether hot or cold, to pursue it by scent while barking constantly to indicate the direction of the chase. As these qualities are complementary, French hunters have crossed the different breeds. The large Anglo-French tricolour breed is the creation of a cross between the foxhound and the Poitevins. They stand 24 to 28 inches tall, with a fairly short snout and large head, flat ears of medium length, a large chest and a straight back. The hair is short, relatively coarse and composed of three distinct colours, with either a black saddle or dispersed black spots. They are adept on harsh terrain; they possess stamina and an excellent gait, a keen sense of smell and a pleasant, resounding bark. Specialized in hunting stag or deer, they can easily adapt to hunting wild boar. The team from the Bonnelles hunting club consists of large Anglo-French tricolours. Like all hunting dogs, after a chase they enjoy a good rest together, nuzzling closely in a tightly-knit pack (following double page). There are two other varieties of Anglo-French tricolours: black and white, and black and orange.

FRENCH TRICOLOUR HOUND

This is the most recent of the French hunting dogs. It was originally bred by Mr. de Falandre during the middle of the twentieth century. The breed is the result of a cross between the large Anglo-French bicolours and Billys and, quite possibly, the Blue Gascony hound. The breed was officially established in 1960. This is a large, graceful and muscular dog. The dogs hunt as a team in orderly fashion. Its rather long head has ears that are somewhat large. It has a deep chest, a sloping back and a long, lifted tail. Its coat is short and soft and made up of three principal colours. Right: Norman Piqu'Hardi, with Mr. Benoît Dulac.

BLOODHOUND

According to legend, this Belgian breed descends from dogs that Saint Hubert brought back to his abbey in the Ardennes after completing a mission in the south of France. This breed is the origin of several other hunting breeds. The Bloodhound was brought to England in the 11th century, where it was rechristened because of its excellent sense of smell. An excellent tracking dog, it is usually used alone, but sometimes is employed in small teams. The dog stands an average of 27 inches at the shoulder. It has a short, tight coat that is usually tan, black and tan or brown and tan in colour. Its large head is typical: the skull is elevated and pointed, covered in a thick wrinkly hide with baggy jowls and long droopy lips. Its bark is powerful.

BILLY

This dog was created during the latter part of the 11th century from a cross between the now non-existent French breeds—the Larye, Céris, Montemboeufs—and to a lesser extent, the Gascon Saintongeois. It is named for property that its creator, Mr. Gaston Hubot du Rivault, owned in Poitou. Fairly large, it measures 24 to 28 inches. It is a well-built dog, strong yet svelte, with the forequarters somewhat higher than the hindquarters. Its finely-featured head has long flat ears that turn somewhat inward. Its short hair is rough to the touch, often on the thick side, and makes for a pleasant coat that is usually uniformly white or coffee-white. In some cases the coat can be off-white or faintly spotted with orange or yellow. This is a deerhunting dog. Right: Chantelouve with Pierrick Le Roux.

ABOVE: Bloodhound, owned by Mr. Creton.

BLUE GASCONY HOUNDS

The Blue Gascony Hound descends from a breed known as the St. Hubert. They were bred originally by the Comte de Foix, Gaston Phébus, who established the line by crossing a number of different hunting breeds that no longer exist. Created during the Middle Ages, they are among the oldest breeds of French hunting dog, and they have changed little since the 14th century. This daring, dynamic, enthusiastic and tenacious breed is divided into four different groups, each notable for its black and white speckled coat that gives it a bluish slate-grey appearance.

BLUE GASCONY GRIFFON

This dog is a cross between a grey wire-haired Griffon and the Blue Gascony Hound. It stands 17 to 21 inches at the shoulder, and is solidly built. Its coarse wiry coat lies mostly flat along the body except at the legs and on the chest where it is slightly curly.

LARGE BLUE GASCONY HOUND

This breed averages between 26 to 30 inches in height, has a long pronounced head, a well-developed chest, a long sloping back and a rich coat that is not too short. Mr. Jacques Baylac has every reason to be proud of Cartouche, who is four years old and a superb example of the breed. True to the breed, he has a fine throaty bark that he employs during the hunt—and on certain special occasions: Cartouche likes to sing along while Mr. and Mrs. Baylac play the accordion. Cartouche is especially fond of this instrument; his singing progressively increases in volume and subtly changes in tone and pitch in near-perfect harmony with Mr. and Mrs. Baylac's playing.

224

ABOVE: Gary, Blue Gascony Griffon, owned by Mr. Allain.

SMALL BLUE GASCONY HOUND

The Small Blue is 21 to 24 inches tall and possesses a fairly long head that is somewhat more delicate than that of its larger cousin, the Blue Gascony Hound. The length of its chest significantly exceeds its width; its back is somewhat long, and its coat is medium, not too short, and plush. This one of the oldest breeds in France.

BLUE GASCONY BASSET

This dog measures 14 to 17 inches at the shoulder. The head is identical in all of its proportions to the Blue Gascony Hound. The coat is somewhat coarse but rich in texture. The dark brown eyes and gentle look of César (right), owned by Mr. Daniel Gibert, are typical of this breed. It is said of the breed that the "dog has four eyes, two of which are marked by a fiery vibrancy", which means that the two patches of tan-coloured fur above the eyebrows make the dog look like it has four eyes.

GRIFFON VENDEEN

The name "Griffon Vendeen" pertains to four different breeds that all issue from a large hunting griffon. The latter is a descendant of the white dogs bred by the royals or perhaps the Royal Court dog, a variety itself of the Royal White dog. These dogs were crossed with the grey Saint Louis breed, the Bresse Griffon and the Fawn Brittany Griffon to yield the Great Griffon Vendeen. The name "griffon" was given to these dogs because of their long, scruffy coats—the hair being very tangled. These breeds are notable for their intelligence and determination. They have long, fine, narrow ears. The back is slightly elevated and the tail is extended and frayed, with the hair on the tail resembling the barbs on a stalk of wheat. The coat is composed either of one colour, such as light brown, grey, tan or white, or of two or three colours. This is a vigorous, courageous, loyal and unwavering animal, possessed with a keen sense of smell and a powerful bark.

GREAT GRIFFON VENDEEN

This dog measures 24 to 26 inches at the shoulder. It is adept at hunting all wild game. Right: Dingo, who belongs to Daniel Boursier, epitomizes the breed's power, nobility and well-balanced proportions. The breed is distinguished by its devotion and steadfastness as a hunting dog.

MEDIUM GRIFFON VENDEEN

The Medium Griffon Vendeen is a slightly smaller hunting dog than the breed from which it is derived. It stands at 20 to 22 inches at the shoulder, between the larger breed and the Basset. It is able to hunt all of the larger game. The elegant silhouette of Douchka de la Combe de Trousse-bois deserves the admiring gaze of Marion Fabre.

ENGLISH FOX HOUND

This English hunting dog descends from a number of different local breeds, who were themselves bred not for their build but for their ability to hunt foxes. The dogs do not officially qualify as belonging to the breed until it has been confirmed that they are descended from at least six generations of foxhounds who have actively and exclusively hunted foxes. These are solid, durable dogs with strong constitutions. They have a powerful build, large skull, long neck, large back and a tail that must taper off. They hunt foxes in the open in an orderly, disciplined pack. Caporol (right) was born in England. Mr. Marcel Thépault has already completed numerous hunting seasons with Caporol and expects to see several more with his longtime companion, who, although ten years old, still retains all of the physical and temperamental qualities of the breed.

ANGLO-FRANÇAIS DE PETITE VÉNERIE

Dr. Emile Guillet, a superb connoisseur of French hunting breeds, described this dog well: "This small, compact dog is a half breed that is well-equipped for its purpose. It lives up to the elegance and distinction that mark the French breeds. It is solid, rapid and has good stamina. The nose and throat are typically French, but what best characterizes it in relation to other breeds of its size is its temperament, which is excellent for hunting large game. Moreover, it is a clever dog that is easy to train." The dog is 19 to 22 inches tall. The coat is short, tight and smooth and composed either of three colours (white, black and tan) or just two (white and black, or white and orange). Edile, three years old, belongs to Mr. Alain Dubois.

BEAGLE-HARRIER

The Beagle-Harrier was created in the late nineteenth century by French hunters. It is a cross between the Harrier-Beagle and the French Medium Griffon Vendeen. Over the years, the original line was found unsatisfactory, and newer lines were created by crossing beagles and harriers. These were developed according to a rigorous breeding scheme introduced by Professor Théret, who holds the Chair of Zootechnology at the École Nationale Veterinaire in Maisons-Alfort. The Central Canine Society approved the scheme, and the breed was officially established in 1980. They are harmonious, well-built dogs with balanced features. They have medium-sized heads and wide, medium-length, almost flat ears. The Beagle-Harrier has a somewhat short, thick coat that is smooth and generally made up of three colours. A multipurpose dog, it can hunt rabbit as well as fox, deer and wild boar.

ABOVE: Beagle-Harrier, owned by Mr. Paltor.

ARTOIS HOUND

This rare breed, a descendant of the bloodhound, almost disappeared in the 20th century. About 20 years ago, a few aficionados decided to reconstitute the breed from a few remaining specimens, which they located after a long search. Thanks to them, the modern Artois Hound closely resembles the original. Measuring 22 to 23 inches at the shoulder, it is a well-constructed dog with a slow, graceful gait. It has a large, strong head, a medium-length back and a pointed tail that is somewhat long and sickle-shaped. Today, it is used primarily to hunt rabbit, although its ancestors were used to hunt deer.

PORCELAINE

This breed was created in the eighteenth century by hunters from Lorraine. It probably descends from the Royal White dog and Swiss hunting dogs of the period. By the 1970s the breed had become so rare that a club was created to preserve it. Three-year-old Elan, shown here with owner Didier Barrier, illustrates the qualities that make this distinguished, small-game hunting dog exceptional in its group. Its rather long head sports fine fleshy ears. It has a fairly long neck, a wide, straight back and a medium-length tail that is slightly curved and tufted at the end. The coat is short, tight, fine and shiny. It is normally white with round orange spots. With a keen sense of smell and an excellent bark, the Porcelaine can hunt anything, but is best at hunting rabbits.

ABOVE: Élégante, Artois Hound, owned by Mrs. Josette Pilat.

FAWN BRITTANY HOUND

This is another of the oldest hunting breeds that were prominent during the Middle Ages. It is descended from a Brittany hunting dog that was a remarkable wolfhound. The breed was for a long time divided into three subtypes: the Griffon, Medium-sized and the Basset (page 242). The medium-sized line has completely disappeared. The Fawn Brittany hound, bony and muscular, gives the impression of vigour and hardiness. Its ears are medium-length and pointed, its neck is muscular, its chest large and tail long and slightly curved. The coat is coarse and wiry, thick but not too long. The colour of the coat varies from golden-red to brick-red.

FAWN BRITTANY GRIFFON

This dog stands between 19 and 22 inches at the shoulder and is used to hunt wild boar and foxes. Bob, who belongs to Mr. Cann, is tough, active and full of character. Endowed with an excellent temperament, it can endure all sorts of hardship, and its hardiness makes it adaptable to all terrains.

GRIFFON NIVERNAIS

This old French breed probably descends from the Bresse Griffon that no longer exists. The Griffon Nivernais is a "barbed" hirsute dog with a coarse coat. It measures 22 to 24 inches at the shoulder. Its head is somewhat long, and it has supple, somewhat hairy medium-length ears. Its back and tail are extended. The coat is wolf-grey, blue-grey or black. The coat is otherwise tan around the jowls, above the eyes and at the extremities. Courageous, if somewhat sad looking, this dog has an exceptional build meant more for endurance than speed. Mr. Guy Lamoureux and Mr. Alain Jullien, who own Gonfleur and Fanfare (right), are never short on praise for these two dogs, whom they appreciate for their keen sense of smell, their superb retrieving qualites and their enthusiasm in the field. They note that the Griffon Nivernais is especially suitable for hunting wild boar or fox.

SMALL BASSET GRIFFON VENDEEN

This small dog, 14 to 15 inches tall, is remarkable for its speed. When let loose on its own in a medium-sized field, the Small Basset Griffon Vendeen is the superlative assistant to any hunter of pheasant or rabbit. It is also an excellent companion with an expressive face and charming manner. Dalton, Eglantine, Emma, Bulle, Gazelle and Houra are the perfect family dogs, as the Fauchereau family can attest. These six little hunters allow the children of the family to pull their tails, their hair and their whiskers without complaint.

FAWN BRITTANY BASSET

At 13 to 15 inches tall, this dog is basically a miniature Fawn Brittany hound whose back is proportionally longer. It is used to flush out wild game. Trained to hunt rabbit, it has a coarse, tough coat that allows it to penetrate the densest thickets and underbrush. Quick and tenacious in action, they are great pets at home due to their calm, affectionate natures.

ABOVE: Fawn Brittany Basset, owned by Mr. Robert Monard.

BASSET ARTÉSIEN NORMAND

This breed was created in the nineteenth century by crossing a Basset d'Artois with a Basset Normand. Ermine des Compagnons des Hautes Erres (right), who belongs to Mr. Christian Dubois, demonstrates the basic basset qualities. The athletic build is elegant and graceful. The Basset Artésien Normand is 12 to 14 inches tall. Its dome-shaped head is adorned with fine, long fleshy ears. Its chest is wide and round, and its back is well-suspended. Its long tail progressively tapers off toward the end and can be extended. The coat is short and composed either of two or three colours. It has a very keen sense of smell, sticks close to the trail and has a fine bark. It is adaptable to all types of wild game but is best suited for rabbit and wild hare. Its gentle temperament, obedience and devotion make it an agreeable companion.

LARGE BASSET GRIFFON VENDEEN

This line was established by Mr. Paul Desamy, who wanted a breed whose size permitted it to pursue and catch wild hare. They are 16 to 17 inches tall.

ABOVE: *Large Basset Griffon Vendeen, owned by Mr. Guy Raffier.*

HARRIER

This English dog was bred, as its name indicates, to "harry" wild hare during the hunt. Several local varieties first appeared during the Middle Ages. English hunters standardised the breed in the nineteenth century. The great cynologist Emile Guillet thought the dog had an average sense of smell and a poor temperament for hunting. He found that the dog lacked initiative and had an erratic bark. In his opinion, it was best suited for fox hunting in open terrain rather than in thick underbrush. French breeding has produced superlative hunters of wild hare. They are sometimes used to hunt fox, deer and wild boar in difficult terrain. The harrier has a smooth, flat coat. The coat is off-white with a spectrum of shades ranging from black to orange. In France the coat is often composed of three colours.

BEAGLE

Although its origins remain controversial, we know that the Beagle was brought to France in the 11th century to hunt wild hare. Two types exist in England: the first is the Standard Beagle, which is unsuitable for hunting; the second is an excellent hunter, but its build does not conform to the standard type. The French Beagle Club has undertaken to create a variety that satisfies the standard form and can also hunt. Their attempts have been very successful. The Beagle has a short, thick coat. It is composed of just about all colours typical of hunting dogs with the one constant being that the tip of the tail is always white. Derby de la Petite Roche, to the left of Jean-Claude Maeso, is quick, active, vigorous and distinguished. Its head is strong without being too heavy, and its ears are flat and round at the tips.

ABOVE: Velina de la Petite Roche, Harrier, owned by Mr. Jean-Claude Maeso.

BASSET HOUND

This British dog is descended from the Basset d'Artois; several types of these dogs were brought to Britain where they were crossed with beagles and bloodhounds. This is the heaviest set of all the bassets. Short legged but well-proportioned, the basset has an appearance of distinction despite its heavy frame. Its size varies from between 13 to 15 inches, and it weighs between 55 and 66 pounds. As we can see from Davidof du Clos d'Egremont and Florentin d'Egremont, who both belong to Mrs. Geneviève Nicolas, the basset has a characteristically large head with a dome shaped skull and heavy folds of skin. Its brown eyes are gentle and sad-looking. The body is long with a fairly wide back. The coat is normally made up of three colours (black, tan and white). Its real forté is hunting, especially foxes, wild boar and wild hare. Indeed, despite its dumpy appearance, the breed is quite agile.

SWISS HOUNDS

Despite a common origin—they are descended from the Blood-hound—these dogs are divided into no less than four different breeds that share a number of features. Essentially, they are distinguished by the colour of their coats. One of the breeds, the Jura Bruno type, differs with respect to a few other features, notably the head, chest, legs and tail. Each of the four breeds includes two varieties that differ in size: 17 to 20 inches for the medium-sized variety and 13 to 16 inches for the smaller sized variety. The dogs belonging to these four breeds have an elongated build. They have a long muzzle, and the ears are folded and coiled. The back is long and straight, and the rather short tail is horizontal and slightly curved either at the rump or towards the tip.

LUCERNE HOUND

The hair is short; the white coat is tinted grey or blue and spotted black.

BERNESE HOUND

As we can see from Cerise de la Suze, who belongs to Mr. Armine Gerber, the coat of this dog is rich and stiff, and coloured black, white and tan.

ABOVE: Lucerne Hound, owned by Mr. Goyat.

JURA HOUND

Bloodhound variety

With Fripon du Val des Feuillants at its head (far right), the well-balanced team of Mr. Michel Aigret exemplifies the characteristics of this breed: a powerful, heavy head with pronounced jowls, a wrinkly forehead and round floppy ears like a Bloodhound. The neck is wide and stout; the back is long and wide; the tail is pointed at the end, and the legs are sturdy. The coat is short and smooth, and its colours are identical to those of the Bruno.

Above: Chiquita des Aquilons du Cholet, Jura Hound (Bruno variety), part of Mr. Henry and Mr. Alain Chopin's pack.

BRUNO DU JURA

Bruno variety

The hair is plush and brown-yellow or brown-red with a black saddle.

SCHWYZ HOUND

White is the background colour of this dog's coat, which usually has large bright orange, yellow orange or reddish orange spots. Following double page: Five medium-sized Schwyz Hounds and a puppy, Filou du Val Durance, are gathered around Mr. Jean-Michel Caponi.

GROUP 7

known—was at first fulfilled by shorthaired dogs known as "brachet". The role was next turned over to dogs of medium-length hair that were trained to *"s'espaignier"*—lie flat on the ground, once they had found the game. The verb *s'espaigner* was first mentioned in the *Book of Hunting* written in the fourteenth century by Gaston Phébus, and it is the etymological origin of the word "spaniel". A long time ago, bird dogs were used to

In the Middle Ages, the ancestors of these dogs were used to locate birds and mark where they were in the bush, usually by lying down and pointing in the right direction. Once the birds were located the hunters would arrive and throw nets over them from behind the dogs. That is how these dogs became known as setters. The role of the "byrde dog"—as it was originally find game, which was then hunted by bow and arrow and later by crossbow. Finally, they were trained to mark the spot where the game was and to crouch down and indicate with their muzzles a bird's exact location. This seventh category is made up of two groups. The first includes breeds from the European Continent, which are further divided into three subgroups depending on the kind of coat they have. The pointing dogs are shorthaired dogs. The spaniels are longhaired or medium-longhaired dogs with silky coats, and the griffons are medium- to longhaired dogs with coarse wiry coats. The second class includes those breeds that are originally from the British Isles: shorthaired pointers and the longhaired setters. These dogs were created from continental breeds and are the result of a cross between the continental dogs and more local breeds. The continental breeds were first introduced to Britain in the sixteenth century.

ITALIAN POINTER

Dea de Cascina Merigo (right), who belongs to Mr. William Courrance, is one of the oldest, if not the oldest, breed of Mediterranean pointer. In the nineteenth century, the breed became a lot heavier and earned the reputation of being rather sluggish hunters. A strict selective breeding programme solved the problem. For over 40 years, breeders have been careful to use only the fastest dogs for maintaining the breed.

Thanks to these efforts, today's pointer has a long graceful, galloping gait. The dog is resilient and has good stamina, which makes it perfect for hunting all types of game, both birds and animals, on all kinds of terrain. A well built dog of about 27 inches and 88 pounds, it has a powerful neck and muscular legs, which give it a vigorous appearance. Its tail is bobbed. Its coat is short and shiny, usually white with either brown or orange spots.

GERMAN WIRE-HAIRED POINTER

This breed was created in the early twentieth century by German breeders who were determined to put an end to the dominance that English hunting breeds enjoyed. To achieve that end, they crossed the Pudelpointer, the Stichelhaar, the Airedale and the German Pointer. The Drahthaar or German Wire-haired Pointer, a coarse-haired dog, was the result of that cocktail and came into being shortly before World War I. It stands an average of 26 inches at the shoulder and is notable for its tight, thick, wiry hair which provides it with the perfect protection. This is a well-proportioned and distinguished looking dog with about equal body length and height. Its dark brown coat is mixed with white and grey patches. Its clear, sad eyes are deeply set in their sockets.

Above: Weimaraner, owned by Mrs. Catherine Buël-Gromaire.

Dog lovers are not in complete agreement about this dog's origins. Some say the dog descends from a medieval grey French dog, several of which were owned by French King Saint Louis. Others say the breed is a cross between the German pointer and other diverse breeds, and was created uniquely by the dukes of Weimar. But everybody agrees that it was the dukes of Weimar who are responsible for establishing the splendid colour of its coat. With its moderately elongated head and its large ears, ample chest, long back and solid muscular build, this dog appears to be graceful and robust. It stands about 24 to 28 inches tall. This excellent pointer is also a remarkable retriever. Barthélemy, Daphné du Dolmen de la Noeveillard and their daughter Gertrude, shown here with Mrs. Catherine Büel-Gromaire, belong to the shorthaired variety that is characterized by a fine, dense coat.

LONGHAIRED WEIMARANER

Right: Ehla and Ekkla, with amber eyes highlighted with silver tints, belong to Mr. Bruno Fasoli. The hair "sticks out" on these dogs and is about 1 to 2 inches long. This variety is also distinguished by a slightly shorter tail.

BOURBONNAIS POINTER

Part of France's national heritage was saved by the concerted efforts of a group of breeders who were very attached to this regional breed. This dog is the result of a judicious selection procedure and was bred from a variety of ancient continental pointers. The reconstitution of the two original colours of the Bourbonnais Pointer caused the breeders considerable trouble. The coat, which is short and thick, can be "peach flowered" (fawn with white speckles) or "wine coloured" (brown with white speckles). Measuring 22 inches at the shoulder, this dog, which has a slightly convex back, is usually born without a tail, but can sometimes be born with a short tail. This light dog is a methodical hunter and usually moves at a gallop. It is best suited for bird hunting, particularly for woodcock and snipe.

Above: Bourbonnais Pointer owned by Mr. Patrice Mallet.

GERMAN SHORT-HAIRED POINTER

The German Short-haired Pointer was created in the second half of the 19th century. Its ancestors were Mediterranean pointers that were later crossed with local breeds. Finding the dog a bit slow, breeders in the early twentieth century tried to lighten the dogs by crossing them with Dobermann Pinschers. Waiting attentively at the feet of Mrs. Maly Taravel and ready for action, Alto and his sons Drilling and Delta, each certified by the office of Clos de Luenas, are powerful, graceful athletes whose fine builds guarantee energy, endurance and speed. The German Short-haired Pointer is about 26 inches tall. Its coat is tight and short as well as coarse. It is usually brown or brown and speckled white, but can sometimes be black or black and speckled white. Its eyes and nose are brown. It also has round medium-length ears that fall around the jowls. This is a bird hunting dog that is at home either in the field, the woods or the marshes.

FRENCH POINTER

This dog is descended from the bird dogs of the Middles Ages, the ancestors of all the breeds in this category. There are two varieties of French Pointer, both of which are able to hunt for long periods of time over difficult terrain. They are adept at hunting quail, pheasant, partridge and wild hare.

GASCONY TYPE

This is the largest of the two existing types and measures 23 to 29 inches. Its head, large but not especially heavy, has medium-length ears that are round and folded at the ends. Its neck is the perfect length; the back is straight, and the tail is bobbed. The coat, thick and plush, is brown or brown and white, or brown with fawn spots. Right: Anky des Messugues Fleuries, owned by Mr. Jean-Pierre Pollart.

PYRENEAN TYPE

Buck du Clos Michaud, who belongs to Mr. Jean Pierre Coeurdray, demonstrates that the Pyrenean variety has exactly the same proportions and characteristics as the Gascony type. But it differs in size—it is about two inches smaller. Its jowls are also less droopy, the ears barely folded and its coat shorter and finer—not to mention its tail, which is also thinner.

HUNGARIAN SHORT-HAIRED POINTER

The Hungarians assert that their national pointer comes from a primitive Hungarian hunting dog, the Pannonie, and a yellow Turkish. Later, the breed was crossed with several other hunting breeds and standardized in the late nineteenth century. An elegant, medium-sized dog of about 24 inches, it has a short fawn coat. Its face is sharp featured, and it has medium length, V-shaped ears. Its back is short and straight. The tail is generally bobbed to about a quarter of its natural length. This dog is calm by nature, has a keen sense of smell and is adaptable and resilient. They make affectionate companions, which is just what Apache de la Bétoule and her daughter Etna (far right) are.

HUNGARIAN WIRE-HAIRED POINTER

Hungarian hunters in the 1930s wanted a dog that would be suited to hunting in heavy underbrush and marshes. The result was a cross between the Hungarian Pointer and the shorthaired Drahthaar. That is how the wirehaired Hungarian Pointer was created, which is slightly bigger and more powerful than its shorthaired cousin. The head of the wirehaired is more angular and bearded than that of the shorthaired. Well protected by its tough, thick coat, the Hungarian wirehaired pointer works well in thickly covered terrain and marshes, but is less rapid when it comes to more favourable terrain. Left: César du Domaine St Hubert, owned by Mr. Jean-Pierre Martin.

ARIÈGE POINTER

This dog descends from a French breed, the Saint-Germain pointer. This is an old breed from southwest France, and it almost disappeared prior to World War II. Fortunately, a couple of dog breeders decided to revive the breed from a few of the remaining specimens whose characteristics still conformed faithfully to the original. The position assumed by Mr. Alain Deteix, that of a sprinter on the block, expresses his determination to complete the revival of this part of France's national heritage. Gouar de la Vallée de la Justale (far right) seems to be enjoying himself. The Ariège pointer is about 26 inches tall. It is solidly built, with a wide, deep chest, a back that is slightly convex in shape and a white coat with brown or orange spots—all features that lend the dog a lot of character. It is suited to hunting partridge or wild hare.

AUVERGNE POINTER

This breed, which dates to the seventeenth century, was the result of selective breeding between local breeds and most definitely the Blue Gascony hound. The Auvergne Pointer is a powerful, strongly built dog, yet it retains a certain lightness. It is at most 25 inches tall. Its fine, short coat, elegant and shiny, belies its rustic appearance. It is coloured black and white and sometimes spotted grey. The tail is bobbed.

ABOVE: Colt de la Font des Passadours, Auvergne Pointer, owned by Mr. Jean Lassandre.

ITALIAN WIRE-HAIRED POINTER

This dog's precise origins are still unknown. This is a large dog (28 inches), solid, rustic and vigorous. The dog's head is bearded and the ears are medium length and triangular in shape. Its neck is strong and muscular. Its coat, made of rough, tight and lightly curly hair, is usually white, white with orange spots or brown. This is an all-terrain hunting dog. The tough coat means that it is at home in thick underbrush and in marshes, even when the water is very cold. When it hunts, it moves with an ample, quick trot that can turn into a pleasant gallop at times. This is an all-purpose hunting dog.

PORTUGUESE POINTER

Its ancestor was an ancient Mediterranean pointer. This breed has developed considerably over the centuries. The breed is not well known in France, and Taro do Odelouca (right), who belongs to Mr. Rochereuil and Mrs. Marquet, is one of the first introduced into France. The dog is 22 inches tall and weighs 60 pounds. The Portuguese Pointer has an excellent build, which endows it with considerable agility. It has a rather small head and medium-length ears that are rounded at the ends. The neck is somewhat long, the back, short, and the hindquarters, fairly squat. The coat is short and stiff and normally a uniform yellow-brown but sometimes spotted.

ABOVE: Happiness Fanny, Italian Wire-haired Pointer, owned by Mr. Hugues Perronny.

BURGOS POINTER

This is one of the oldest pointing breeds, but its origins remain unknown. Ton (below), who belongs to Mr. Pascal Moreira, is of average size for his breed—about 26 inches—and of medium build; this dog gives an impression of power and hardiness. The Burgos pointer has a large, solid head with long dangling ears. The look in its chestnut eyes is gentle and slightly melancholy. The coat is tight, short and smooth. It is normally white with liver-coloured spots. The tail is bobbed to about one-third to one-half its natural length. This dog is suited both for fowl and wild game. Its favourite prey is the partridge. In action, its gait is long, powerful and efficient.

SAINT-GERMAIN POINTER

The breed was created in the mid-nineteenth century by crossing French pointers with other pointing breeds. This is an elegant, well-proportioned dog. Dick du Bois d'Heilly, owned by Mr. Stanislas d'Argentre, has large golden-yellow eyes, which give the breed its frank and gentle appearance. This is a very well-tempered dog who loves to retrieve, often pouncing on any object that can be brought to its master.

The ears of the Saint-Germain are smaller than the older breed, the French pointer, but longer than that of the other pointing dogs. The neck is fairly long, the chest is wide and the back is short and straight. The fur is short and never coarse, while the coat itself is off-white with orange spots.

ABOVE: Ton, Burgos Pointer, owned by Mr. Pascal Moreira.

BLUE PICARDY SPANIEL

This breed is a cross between a Picard Spaniel and a Gordon Setter. It became an official breed in its own right during the period between the two World Wars. Attila de la Valée de l'Ysieux (right), who belongs to Mr. Lucien Bernard, is a perfect example of the breed. The Picard blue has a low-set build, and its appearance is very similar to the Picard Spaniel except that its hair is flat and wavy, and a speckled grey-black colour. Its fur is magnificent, and its bluish tint gives the dog's shape a more rustic aspect than that of the Picard. It measures 24 inches and has an attractive head framed by somewhat thick ears that are beautifully fringed. Its back is fairly short. Its legs are also well furnished with tassel-like fur. Tireless and good-tempered, this dog can hunt most game. Its keen sense of smell makes it an excellent hunter of woodcock.

BRITTANY SPANIEL

Among its ancestors was a small dog that lived in Brittany during the twelfth century. The descendants of this dog were used in the nineteenth century by woodcock hunters from Argoat. When they were crossed with hunting dogs, the result was the Brittany Spaniel. This little dog is fearless, quick, intelligent, dynamic and always alert. Flicka de Saint-Tugen and Caouette de Saint-Tugen (right) are always ready when Mr. Maurice Marchand gives them the call. This dog stands at a maximum of 20 inches, and has a round head and a muzzle with elevated lips. Its ears are short and somewhat fringed. Compact and stocky, it has a straight back and relatively round features. The tail varies in size from very short to fairly long. The coat is either straight or wavy and coloured white and orange, white and brown, or black and white. This is one of the most popular French hunting dogs. It has an excellent sense of smell, is tireless and can endure all conditions and climates.

FRENCH SPANIEL

Although it descends from the bird dogs of the Middle Ages, the precise genealogy of this breed remains uncertain. However, it is known that this dog is the origin of several other breeds. Friendly and gentle, this is a loyal and devoted dog. This faithfulness explains the impatience with which Dervin rushes to join his master, Mr. Monceau de Lafitte, who divides his attention equally between Dervin and Titien (see following double page).

The purity of this breed of dog is responsible for its pleasing, harmonious build. A medium-sized dog, it holds its well-sculpted head proudly. The dog's amber coloured eyes reflect intelligence. Its coat is made up of straight fur that is silky and covers the body abundantly. It is white with irregular brown spots. This dog can hunt any kind of wild game, whether animal or fowl, over any kind of terrain, be it an open field or a marsh.

PICARDY SPANIEL

Echo de la Vallée Broutin waits calmly but with anticipation for the return of his master, Mr. Pascal Lempereur, because he wants to go hunting for wild hare or marsh mallard. The Picard Spaniel is a very adaptable dog and can hunt on all kinds of terrain. A tenacious breed, it will carefully cover an entire area, leaving not a square foot unexamined. At 24 inches, it has a stocky appearance. Its head is framed by low-set ears, and its look is serious. Its back is medium length. Its paws are fringed, and its tail, adorned with silky fur, is slightly curved. Its fur is thick, plush and silky. The coat is grey with large spots of brown, giving it a rather distinguished appearance.

Drakkar de la Verderie du Quesney (right), obediently seated beside Mr. André Joulot, owes its near-perfect coat, not to mention its appealing form, to the efforts of a few Norman breeders. Indeed, this ancient French breed, a cross between a French Spaniel and an Irish Water Spaniel, had almost become extinct. The breed has today nearly completely recovered. Of medium size, it is squat yet vigorous. Its head is topped with a curly tuft of fur that stands almost straight up. Its ears also have long silky fur that runs right up to the tuft making the head almost look like it is framed by a wig. Its tail is bobbed. Its curly coat, though somewhat gruff, is brown or brown and porcelain grey and with light brown highlights. Its love of the water makes it an excellent duck hunter. But its energy and vigour make it adaptable to all kinds of wild game.

MUNSTERLANDER

The Münsterländer comes in two varieties, which have a few features in common, such as an aristocratic head, a deep chest and a straight back. The dog is at home on all types of terrain and can hunt any kind of game. It is notable for being a methodical stalker. The large Münsterländer stands 22 to 23 inches tall in comparison with the smaller variety, which stands 20 to 22 inches tall. The coat is white with black or maroon spots, while the smaller of the two has a coat that is white and brown or brown-maroon.

GERMAN LONGHAIRED POINTER

Although this breed dates back several centuries, it was eschewed by German hunters in favour of the German Pointer and the Drahthaar. Today, the breed is enjoying something of a comeback in its native land but is still largely unknown outside Germany. Capone du Buisson de Choisel hunts with Mr. Alfred Vallet in the Chevreuse valley, on the same land where members of the French royalty once hunted. He is seen here demonstrating how big this longhaired hunting dog actually is— about 26 inches. The dog is also robust and muscular, with an elongated head, and a straight, short back. Its long hair is straight and fringed at the paws. The coat is brown.

ABOVE: Cook du Clos des Hortioux, Münsterländer, owned by Miss Géraldine Ross.

FRENCH WIRE-HAIRED POINTING GRIFFON

This dog's ancestors were used for hunting in ancient times. The modern breed was established by a Dutchman, Mr. Korthals, from a cross between several breeds including the German, Belgian, Dutch and French griffons. The dog fell out of favour after the death of Mr. Korthals. French breeders appreciated the dog's qualities and continued the breed. Vasco, who belongs to Mr. Lesiourd, is an excellent example of this breed. This is a medium-sized dog (23 inches). Its appearance is a bit rustic but nevertheless pleasant. Its long large head is adorned with tufted fur, with a beard, moustache and bushy eyebrows, which almost cover its eyes. The expression is one of fidelity and reliability. Its iron-grey coat is covered with brown spots and its fur is wiry and tough and resembles the fur of a wild boar. Together, these characteristics protect the dog from cold and brambles, and make it ideal for hunting all kinds of wild game, anywhere and at any time of the year.

SLOVAKIAN WIRE-HAIRED POINTING GRIFFON

The exact origins of this dog are unknown, but it enjoys an excellent reputation in Slovakia where the breed was created. This is a large dog that can reach up to 27 inches in size. It is attentive and powerful, and can hunt both in woods and in marshes. It is also notable for its obedience. The Slovaks often use it as a bloodhound to track wounded game. Its powerfully shaped head sports a strong jawline and medium length ears that are round and floppy. The neck is set back on the shoulders; its back is straight and firm and its medium-sized tail is bobbed about halfway down and extended. The fur is on average about 1½ inches long and coloured silver-grey without spots, or grey with dark spots. Far right: Bruna Rissa, owned by Mrs. Lucette Geffroy.

ENGLISH POINTER

This breed is descended from Iberian pointing dogs that were brought to England during the eighteenth century. After crossings between local breeds and perhaps continental pointers, the breed was established in the late nineteenth century. Its build is harmonious and it gives the impression of strength and agility. A good-sized dog, it is muscular and lithe of limb. The coat is fine and short, shiny and coloured yellow and white, orange and white, brown and white, or black and white. This is a thorough hunter who explores every inch of the terrain and is at its best in wide open spaces. Woodcock, quail and pheasant are its favourite game.

ABOVE: Émeraude des Buveurs d'Air, Pointer, owned by Mr. Lesiourd.

GORDON SETTER

This athletic breed was established in Scotland toward the end of the eighteenth century by the Earl of Gordon. It has the long, galloping gait of a horse. The finely chiseled features of its head are remarkable. Its ears accentuate its aristocratic appearance giving it a lively, intelligent demeanour. Its coat is a deep coal-black with tan markings. The fur is of medium length, smooth along the body but short and soft around the head. Its ears, stomach and hind paws are fringed. Conscientious, this dog covers the terrain scrupulously. Intelligent and hardy, the dog paces itself well. It is good at hunting all sorts of game, but its strong point is the woodcock. Banco, being admired here by Elsie Mate Hannsfield and Fee Black du Val de Chauffour, is a remarkable hunting dog and the leader of a team of eight Gordons belonging to Mr. Jean-Dominique Dvorak.

IRISH SETTER

This is the oldest setter breed from the British Isles. Its distant origins remain unclear, but it is thought that the breed descended from continental pointers of possible Mediterranean origin. Vent d'ouest du Hobereau du Clos des Pins (right), who belongs to Mrs. Rittalis, has a noble disposition and a friendly appearance, which is typical of the Irish setter. This is a sporty, intelligent breed whose robustness, adaptability and endurance make it a perfect hunting dog. This dog performs well either in the open, or on wooded or marshy terrain. It has a remarkably keen sense of smell. The dog's build gives it an appearance of graceful power. The head has an excellent shape. Its eyes are dark, and its nose is brown or chestnut. The coat is a beautiful fawn-red with straight soft fur. Its stomach, tail and hind paws are fringed with long hair. This is a fantastic dog that is the joy of every hunter and his family.

ENGLISH SETTER

The English Setter owes its existence to an English breeder named Mr. Laverack who established the breed in the second half of the nineteenth century. The first English Setters reached France in the late 19th century. A medium-sized dog, its coat is silky with long tassels covering the paws and tail. The coat can be coloured white and black, orange and white, white and brown, or black, white and brown. This dog has a keen sense of smell and is excellent for hunting all kinds of game, but it is at its best hunting woodcock in wooded areas. Its style of hunting is brilliant and is characterized by a smooth, low-angled gait alternating with striking short stops, all of which make it a joy to watch in action.

ABOVE: Coca de l'Étoile de Moreuil, English Setter, owned by M. Olivier Bouchet.

RETRIEVERS
FLUSHING DOGS
AND WATER DOGS

This category includes breeds used for highly specific tasks. These tasks require a certain aptitude and breeding altogether different from the standard hunting breeds. The first subgroup includes breeds used to retrieve wounded or dead game on land or in water. These dogs belong to breeds that are capable not only of retrieving small game such as woodcock and partridge but also larger game such as pheasant and wild hare. Some of these breeds have

highly specialized abilities, which make them adaptable to more unusual purposes. These abilities depend on certain qualities, in particular a keen sense of sight and smell, attentiveness, a good sense of direction, determination, courage and a gentle disposition. These qualities make them especially useful as seeing-eye dogs, dogs trained for aiding disabled individuals and dogs trained by the police and customs officials for detecting drugs and explosives. The second subgroup includes dogs bred to detect and flush out wild game, whether it be in the field, in thick underbrush or in heavily wooded areas. They are often referred to by the term broussailleur, or bush dog. Originally they were bred only for the purpose of flushing out wild game. The job of pursuing and retrieving the game was reserved for other breeds. Today, most of these breeds are trained to undertake all three tasks. The third subgroup includes those breeds that are specialized in hunting animals and waterfowl either by the sea, along rivers or in swamps and marsh land. This type of game includes different varieties of waterfowl, such as duck, waders (snipe, plover, curlew) and grouse and coot. All the dogs belonging to these breeds love water. They take great pleasure in diving into water regardless of the temperature. That's because they have thick, multi-layered coats that adequately protect them from freezing temperatures.

LABRADOR RETRIEVER

Dance With Me de Saint-Urbain (right) has adopted an attitude that demonstrates this breed's attachment to its masters, in this case Mr. Michel Germain. The breed is descended from the Saint-John which was brought to England from Newfoundland by English sailors at the end of the 18th century. The remarkable characteristics of this dog made it a favourite among English breeders, who for sixty years instituted a strict breeding programme that included only the finest specimens. The breed was formally established only at the end of the nineteenth century. This dog is above all a hunting dog whose hardiness makes it adaptable to all sorts of game. It is a superb retriever, especially in water. A medium-sized dog, it is solidly built, compact and strong. The coat is short. The tail is medium length, tapered to a point and extended directly from the back. The colour of the coat is black, brown or yellow. This active dog is known to be "gentle of tooth," as it retrieves game without damaging it.

FLAT-COATED RETRIEVER

This medium-sized breed is the product of a careful breeding programme implemented in the late 19th century by British breeders, who wanted to create an English dog that specialized in retrieving wild game from all types of terrain. They crossed a North American breed from the region around the Saint Lawrence River with the Irish setter. The North American breed was chosen because of its strong build and its love of water. The dog measures an average 24 inches in size and weighs about 75 pounds. It has an elongated head with a flat skull, small ears and a powerful jaw. Its coat is fine but thick and flat. The colour is black or brown, and the paws and tail are heavily fringed. Active and alert, this is a natural-born hunter with a remarkably keen sense of smell. It is able to hunt on all kinds of terrain but is best in marshland, as it is an exceptional swimmer. Its patience, obedience and lively disposition make it a wonderful companion.

NOVA SCOTIA DUCK TOLLING RETRIEVER

The ancestry of this dog has not yet been precisely determined. The breed originated in Nova Scotia, a province of Canada situated off the Atlantic seacoast near the United States. The dog specializes in retrieving duck. It is medium-sized—a maximum 20 inches for around 50 pounds—and has a compact and muscular body. Its head is notable for its large size, streamlined muzzle and triangular shaped ears of medium length. When in action, the tail is raised and rolled up. It has a double layered water resistant coat. The coat can be any shade of colour ranging from red to orange. Despite a somewhat dumpy appearance, the dog is actually very agile. It is a determined and energetic duck hunter, and it stalks its prey with great speed. During the chase, it constantly wags its tail. When not hunting, the dog is a great companion, as demonstrated by Ducky Ardunacres, pictured here with Mrs. Léveillé-Nizerolle.

CHESAPEAKE BAY RETRIEVER

The origins of this dog are a matter of controversy among dog lovers. There are two different versions: some say the breed descended from a primitive North American strain that developed over the centuries. For others, the breed did not come into being until the nineteenth century and was the result of a cross between the Newfoundland and local Maryland breeds. What is certain, however, is that the Chesapeake Bay retriever is an excellent swimmer. The dog is 23 to 27 inches in size and about 65 pounds. Like Chesabay Cruiser, called Duck, who belongs to Mr. Jean-Louis Pigal, these dogs have large round heads and small pendulous ears. The neck is very muscular, and its "wild hare feet" are webbed and large. Its coat, with short straight fur, can be any colour, ranging from dark brown to light tan or even straw. It has an excellent sense of smell.

GOLDEN RETRIEVER

Despite the innumerable controversies surrounding the origins of this breed, it seems certain that it was created at the end of the nineteenth century by an English breeder who crossed flat-haired retrievers with the Irish setter. Agile, with a great love of water, this is a multipurpose hunting dog. Its disposition is calm and gentle. A medium-sized dog, the golden retriever is perfectly proportioned. Its head is distinguished by a snout that ends abruptly, a black nose, and ears that are medium-sized and floppy. The expression on its face is gentle and friendly. The coat is thick, with silky, straight fur. It paws are fringed, as is its tail, which falls directly from its back. The colour of the coat ranges from cream to deep g o l d e n without any trace of red.

RHODESIAN RIDGEBACK

This dog is descended from a Rhodesian breed that was crossed with European breeds brought from Europe by the Boers. The result was a large South African dog used to track lions, flush them out and chase them in the direction of the hunters. A crest of hair runs along the dog's back in the opposite direction from the rest of the coat and gives the dog its name. Standing 27 inches tall, this large dog is strong, muscular, active and has excellent endurance. The dog accelerates rapidly and is remarkably calm during the chase. Asimbothanda didn't hesitate to jump 8 feet to join his master, Mr. Bruno Hachet, to reach the roof where he was working. Detached and intelligent, the Rhodesian Ridgeback has an excellent sense of smell, which makes him a superb tracking dog, while his detachment makes him perfect for hunting wild boar and deer.

ABOVE: Sunbeam Gentle V.H. Heideduin, Golden Retriever, owned by Mrs. Marja Kuyf-Jochemus.

CLUMBER SPANIEL

The ancestors of this breed were British spaniels that were chosen for being heavy-boned. It owes its name to Clumber Castle, which is located in the county of Nottingham. There, the dukes of Newcastle established a kennel that housed a large number of the breed. Its long body is strong and low-set and this gives it the appearance of being massive and slow, which is not at all the case. In fact, this is a very active dog. Measuring on average 19 inches and 72 pounds, it has a square-shaped powerful head with a wide brow. Its eyes are somewhat deep-set, which gives it a pensive air. The coat is abundant, tight and silky. The colour is white with yellow marks. Due to its determination, the Clumber excels in finding wild game in heavy underbrush. Its stable disposition also makes it an agreeable companion. Mr. Alain Jacq is rightly proud of Basile de Floriac, whose sire was the original stud used in breeding the French variety before he was hit by a car and killed.

This breed was created in the twentieth century from the English Cocker by American breeders who desired a smaller version of the dog with longer hair. Eli-France du Clos d'Aldebaran, who belongs to Mr. Jean Diot but is seen here in the arms of Miss Pascale Cauche, is the epitome of this breed: he has a finely chiseled head with a foreshortened muzzle that makes the head look square in comparison to the English Cocker. The fur is short and soft on the head, of medium length on the body and beautifully fringed around the ears, chest, stomach and paws. The tail is bobbed. The coat can be all one colour, ranging from black to any other tint, or it can have two well defined and well separated colours. Due to its graceful form, the American Cocker is a true athlete, solidly built and endowed with a keen sense of smell. Rapid and tireless, this dog loves to hunt. It is also intelligent and "bubbly", its natural good humour and joyfulness making it a veritable clown. The dog is small enough to go anywhere and is a pleasant travelling companion. Lady, the heroine of the cartoon Lady and the Tramp, made this American breed enormously popular.

SUSSEX SPANIEL

An English hunter who lived in the county of Sussex created this breed in the early nineteenth century. He desired a dog that would be good at flushing out game. He wanted a vigorous dog that wasn't too fast but had a powerful bark, so that the hunter could follow the chase through the most densely wooded terrain.
The result was achieved by crossing several spaniel breeds.
The dog is about 16 inches tall and 45 pounds. This is a heavy, well-built dog with large thick ears and a slightly curved neck. Its abundant flat fur makes for a beautiful brown coat. Active, energetic and strong, the dog has an easygoing disposition and a characteristic rolling stride. It is also an extremely agreeable companion, as demonstrated by the complicity between Victoria du Gallet Doré and Mrs. Dominique Cornet-Gougon (far right).

FIELD SPANIEL

This breed is fairly scarce in France. The Field Spaniel differs from the English Cocker in that its head is more heavyset and its muzzle more pronounced. The body is also longer, and the tail hangs lower. Calm, robust and quick, this hunting dog excels in the field and is excellent both at flushing out wild game and retrieving.

Above: Muharraq Sir Galahad, Field Spaniel, owned by Miss Gaëlle Teze.

ENGLISH SPRINGER SPANIEL

This dog, which belongs to the large English Spaniel family. This is the largest spaniel bred to hunt in either the fields or woods. At 20 inches, it has a large, beautifully shaped and somewhat round head with finely fringed ears. The tail, also fringed, wags often, reflecting the dog's liveliness and love of life. The coat is straight and tight, protecting it from inclement weather, and coloured either black and white or brown and white. It sometimes has three colours, the third being dark tan. A natural-born hunter, the English Springer is large and solidly built, which means it can cover large areas with great speed, often creating the impression that it is flying over the land. Thanks to its powerful jaws, it is able to retrieve heavy or large game. This docile dog is adaptable to all lifestyles and is a great family dog.

WELSH SPRINGER SPANIEL

This breed is the result of a careful breeding programme implemented during the nineteenth century aimed at obtaining the characteristics that are specific to the Welsh Springer: great endurance, courage and insurmountable energy, which make it a multipurpose dog. It differs from the English Springer Spaniel in its smaller size (by about 1 inch), its large floppy ears—as demonstrated here by Fidji, seen in the arms of Mathias Catala—and the colour of its coat, which is bright red and white. Quick, active and tireless, the Welsh Springer is an enterprising breed.

ABOVE: Folk du Pigeonnier Bruyères, English Springer, owned by Mrs. Fabienne Courtel.

SPANISH WATER DOG

This dog is common in southern Spain. As one can see from Darro de Ubrique, who belongs to Mr. Ricardo Taus Hortal (right), this is a rustic-looking, well-proportioned dog. Its well-textured coat makes it adaptable to both dry and damp environments, which makes it perfect for the marshy terrain of Andalusia. Loyal, good tempered and hard working, this dog belongs to a breed that has been provisionally recognized by the World Canine Organisation. A period of ten years must pass before a scientific committee can officially establish the breed, which requires that it be free of any hereditary defects.

PORTUGUESE WATER DOG

The build of the Portuguese Water Dog indicates its close kinship with the barbet, which is not surprising given that both breeds are derived from a Middle Eastern dog that was brought to Spain during the Arab invasion and occupation of the Iberian peninsula. This medium-sized dog is well constructed with a large head, broad chest, short back and tail that is tufted at the end. The coat is either long and lightly curled or short with tight cylindrical curls. The coat is usually uniformly black, but it can also be uniformly brown or white, or black and white or brown and white. Alert, impetuous and hardy, the Portuguese water dog has excellent vision and a keen sense of smell.

ABOVE: *Nosferatu de Montalin, Portuguese Water Dog, owned by Mr. Pierre Botijo de Oliveira.*

ENGLISH COCKER SPANIEL

Continental Spaniels were first introduced to the British Isles in the late fifteenth century. They were crossed with local breeds to create many eclectic British spaniel breeds. The English Cocker is the result of careful breeding between smaller-sized spaniels. The breed was introduced to France at the end of the nineteenth century. Athletic and aristocratic, this dog is on average 16 inches tall and weighs about 30 pounds. It is an energetic hunter that loves water and loves to retrieve. Espion and Fabiolo (black dogs), Full Up and Dhango (blue dogs) as well as Varec (red dog), illustrate the variety of colours of English Cockers. These dogs belong to Mrs. Catherine Jacquier-Graveleau. The remarkable range of colours and silky coat, not to mention well-balanced disposition, tenacity in flushing out game from the most inaccessible places and sociable nature, make this dog popular as a hunter and companion. It is the hero of the French comic book series *Boule et Bill*.

IRISH WATER SPANIEL

This breed is a cross between the Irish Setter and Standard Poodles. The precise date at which the cross occurred has not been established. A medium-sized dog, its oily coat is made of thick curls, which resemble the fleece of a sheep. The coat is coloured brown but of an unusual tint particular to the breed. Eliot des Monts de Caux (right) has the characteristic head of the Irish Water Spaniel: a long muzzle that is somewhat square and pronounced, a dome-shaped forehead covered in long curls that resemble a wig, a brown nose that is well developed, and very long round ears that hang around the neck. Enthusiastic, this dog is particularly adapted to hunting fowl, but it is also able to hunt other game.

FRISIAN WATER DOG

This breed has existed in the Netherlands for centuries. Although a bird dog, it was originally used to hunt otter, which were especially prevalent in Frisia, a flat region bordering the North Sea. It stands 24 inches tall and is a robustly built dog. Its head is sharply featured, and its body is covered by a thickly curled coat (except for the head and paws). The curls are made of firm, thick fur and are coloured either a uniform black or brown, or black with white spots or brown with white spots. A courageous and determined dog, it has a calm but stubborn character that makes it perfect for keeping an unflagging and vigilant guard.

318

ABOVE: Enkel Fan It Gouden Wetterhart, Frisian Water Dog, owned by Mr. J-J Dupont.

The ancestors of this dog guarded herds in North Africa. The Arabs introduced the breed to France, where it was first established in the south-west of the country. Peasants in the Middle Ages also used it to guard their herds. After discovering its ability as a hunting dog, they undertook to improve these qualities. When hunting rights were extended to the general population after the Revolution, the Barbet became the constant companion of hunters, who used it in marshland. The dog's popularity waned after World War I, and the breed almost disappeared. Today, it is making a successful comeback. Standing at a maximum of 20 inches tall, its thick woolly coat protects it from both the water and the cold, which is why it is excellent for hunting in marshy areas. The fur on its head has a tendency to fall over and almost completely cover its eyes. The coat can be either uniformly coloured black, grey, brown, fawn or white, or it can be a mix of colours.

Colombo Noir des Marécages du Prince, called Cyrus for short, always amazes Mrs. Françoise Couturas by his special talent: when the dog is exploring a river or a marsh, it has an extraordinary ability to catch fish.

COMPANION AND TOY DOGS

This category includes breeds that were developed for purposes of companionship, rather than to perform a specific function. These dogs are bred to play the role of friend and confidant to their master, to provide comfort to the lonely and reassurance and affection to family members. Dogs in this category thus play a considerable and indispensable social service in our contemporary urban environments.

Although the distinguishing feature of these dogs may be their small size, the main characteristic for which they were bred was not a convenient morphology but rather an attentive and genial disposition. As Professor Raymond Triquet explains: "There is, of course, no one single type of lap dog. The dogs in this category resemble each other only in that they are readily amenable to providing their masters with the pleasure of their company."

323

HAVANESE BICHON

Is it because this is the largest of the Bichon breeds, at 14 and 20 pounds, that Maiden Effort's Velasquez is so happy to dominate her owner, Mrs. Nicole Perchet? It is certainly not because this Havanese is a little despot. On the contrary: although the Havanese Bichon can be assertive, it remains an affectionate and obedient companion. It has a large flat head with large dark eyes that are usually black and a tapered muzzle with flat cheeks. The coat is made of soft tufted fur that is slightly curled at the ends. Its coat is occasionally white but usually dark beige or light brown, like a cigar. That is why this dog, of Mediterranean origin and unusually fastidious, was named after the "Havana".

BICHON BOLOGNESE

Descended from the Maltese, this Italian breed was a favourite of the Medici. It was widely popular throughout Italy during the Renaissance, after which its popularity declined, and the breed was increasingly forgotten. Today, even in Italy, there remain only a few specimens of the breed. Its long white fur and abundant curls give many people the impression that the dog requires a lot of upkeep. But the beautiful coat of this small dog, who measures 11 to 12 inches tall and weighs about 6½ to 9 pounds, requires only a daily brushing to maintain its fine lustre. This is a playful affectionate dog who is always alert and on guard when he senses that something is up

ABOVE: *Genepy du Mont-Aiguille, Bichon Bolognese, owned by Mrs. Laurence Fluchaud.*

BICHON FRISÉ

This breed was created in France during the fifteenth century from a cross between the Maltese and the poodle. This was Henri III's favourite dog, and the breed was enormously popular among European nobility. It was at this time that the verb bichonner, or "dress up," was coined. It referred to the excessive care that noblewomen lavished on their dogs. The breed fell out of fashion after World War I but was revived after the end of World War II through the efforts of several French and Belgian breeders. As a result, the breed is officially recognized as being both French and Belgian. This is a robust dog measuring about 11 to 12 inches and is noted for its proud, almost haughty, disposition. It has expressive eyes and a jet-black nose, the ears hang down and are covered with fine curly fur. The fur elsewhere is also fine, silky and tightly curled; the coat is completely white in colour but requires little maintenance.

MALTESE BICHON

This breed is the oldest in the Bichon family. The breed originated in Egypt and eventually spread throughout the Mediterranean. It was most popular in Italy during the Middle Ages. The dog is 8 to 10 inches tall and weighs 6½ to 9 pounds. That makes it the smallest of the Bichon breeds. This small dog has a long, thin body covered with very long, silky, shiny fur. This bestows upon the dog an elegant, if uniform appearance. Its long white coat requires regular brushing. Like all the other Bichon breeds, the Maltese is obedient, affectionate and very alert. Right: Yvon Perrin, holding Solitaire Abbyat du Fantôme von Harlekin at arm's length, with Feeling du Fantôme von Harlekin on his lap.

ABOVE: Bichon Frisé, owned by Mrs. Sylvie Dordet.

MADAGASCAR

A shipwreck off the coast of Madagascar in the sixteenth century is at the origin of this breed from Madagascar. The survivors had a few Maltese dogs with them for companionship. The sailors rescued the dogs and later bred them with local toy breeds. Their cotton-ball tail, and the fact that the breed emerged in a region near Tuléar, gave the breed the French version of its name, the Coton de Tuléar. This is a small breed well suited for city living. It is 12 inches tall and weighs about 12 pounds. The head is triangular in shape and nicely coiffed. The dangling ears are thin, and the nose is jet black with flared nostrils. As evidenced by Diabolo Swing Five O'Clock and Evinrude du Petit Dan, seated on the knees of Nathalie and Goran Brabani-Brkic, this dog has a marvellous pure white coat made of long, fine, slightly wavy fur. It has an affectionate, playful character and is always in good spirits. The Madagascar is an active dog with an infectious love of life.

POODLE

This French breed was developed in the Middle Ages and descends from the Barbet, a bird dog. The poodle became a favourite among ladies of the French royal court in the seventeenth century. Later, the dog also became popular among the lower echelons of society and achieved its widest popularity in the nineteenth century. The breed then found favour in Anglo-Saxon countries, especially in the United States. There, it is one of the three breeds with the largest number of annually registered births, according to the American Kennel Club. This is a harmoniously built, well-proportioned dog. The coat is characteristically curly, with abundant fine and woolly fur. Although somewhat rare today, there is a type of poodle known as the "cordé," after its almost rope like locks of nearly equal length. The coat is generally uniformly white, black, brown, apricot or grey. Originally bred as a hunting dog adapted to marshy terrain, the wonderful

disposition of this dog, with its proverbial fidelity, so beautifully depicted in Hector Malot's novel, *Sans Famille,* along with its vivacity, dynamism, endurance, playful character and intelligence, have made the poodle the most popular French breed. There are four different types of poodle distinguished by size.

STANDARD POODLE

Measures 18 to 23 inches. Many owners of this breed often refer to it as the "royal poodle". Calynka, a large apricot-colored poodle, who belongs to Mrs. Alagiraude, is pictured with Help Me Golden du Chateâu de Mesne, who is just two months old (preceding double page).

MEDIUM-SIZED POODLE

Measures 14 to 18 inches.

TOY POODLE

Under 11 inches (ideally, under 10 inches). Right: Bambi de l'Orée de Sologne, belonging to Mrs. Christiane Couroux.

LITTLE LION DOG

This breed belongs to the Bichon family. Its fur is cropped in the same style as a poodle, with the tail ending in a tuft. The coat makes it look like a little lion. The fur is long and wavy and never curly. The coat can be any colour, but white, yellow and black are the most common. Lively, intelligent and affectionate, it alerts its master with a sharp continuous bark the second it senses danger. Above: Fhidias Samson de l'Ancien Relais, owned by Mr. Wilfrid Vattement.

MINIATURE POODLE

Measures 11 to 14 inches.

SMALL BELGIAN DOGS

Although these dogs are judged as separate breeds at dog shows due to the fact that the World Canine Organisation has established an independent standard for each, in reality these dogs technically belong to the same breed. There are three varieties, distinguished by the colour and nature of their coats. That's why they are often referred to collectively by the same affectionate epithet—the "little Belgians". These griffons are descended from ratters, who were originally bred for their ability to exterminate the vermin and rodents that infested stables. Intelligent, agile and robust, they have an appealing and elegant build. The head is large and round, and the ears are straight and always pointed. The tail is bobbed very short.

BRUSSELS GRIFFON

The stiff, wiry fur is red in colour. Endor's Crazy About You, who belongs to Mrs. Elyanne Villemot-Braun, is agreeable, obedient and very affectionate, like all the little Belgians.

BRABANT GRIFFON

This dog's coat is either a uniform red, or black and tan. As Mr. Stéphane Segal demonstrates here with Daphné de la Romance du Mal Aimé, owned by Mrs. Marie-France Wall, the compact size of the Brabant Griffons makes it easy to take them anywhere. Their almost human expression also makes them irresistible.

BELGIAN GRIFFON

This dog's fur is wiry, dishevelled and of medium length. The coat is uniformly coloured black or coloured black and tan or black and red. These are popular lap dogs.
Below: Enzo de la Romance du Mal Aimé owned by Mrs. Marie-France Wall.

HAIRLESS DOGS

It was for reasons of simplicity that the originators of the different categories of dog breeds established the category of the "hairless breeds." In fact, no single breed is completely hairless, and the dogs belonging to this category have a bit of fur on their heads and at the end of their tails.

MEXICAN HAIRLESS

Originally from Mexico, this is a very ancient breed. Its name was given to it by the Incas, who considered it the living incarnation of Xolotl, the God of the Earth. Xolotl's task was to accompany souls of the dead to their final destination. It is therefore somewhat paradoxical that given how much they venerated this breed, the Incas also considered the dogs to be something of a delicacy, which they served up enthusiastically during festivals. The breed is almost completely hairless except for a few hairs on its head and at the end of its tail. The dog has a gracious disposition. Its skin is smooth and soft to the touch and is generally dark brown, elephant grey, grey-black or black. This is the only dog to perspire through its skin, which explains why it only rarely exposes its tongue. The dog is very dignified and reserved among strangers. But one can see from B'Luna, seated here on the lap of Mr. Pierre Maisonneuve, that the Mexican Hairless is by nature an outgoing, dynamic and sociable dog. It is perfectly suited to urban environments because it is remarkably clean and hardly ever barks.

The Chihuahua is descended from a primitive breed that accompanied the Toltecs when they settled in Mexico during the tenth century. The dog later met the same fate as the Aztecs, who maintained the breed, becoming a victim of the Conquistadors during the sixteenth century. A few survived among the peasants in isolated areas of what is today the state of Chihuahua, next to the United States border. It was there that American breeders rediscovered the dog in the nineteenth century. They appreciated the breed and dubbed it the Chihuahua, after the state where it was discovered. The dog is reputed to be the smallest breed in the world, weighing from 2 to $2^1/_2$ pounds. Contrary to its fragile appearance and small size, the Chihuahua is alert, active and tough. It has no fear of confronting dogs that are much larger in size. Its head is round, and its muzzle is short and somewhat pointed with a black nose. The tail is curled up on the back. There are two varieties of Chihuahua that differ only with respect to the fur. Mrs. Germaine Blondel is seen here holding one of each. On the left, Carino Desierto del Perro, a smooth-haired variety, with tight and shiny fur. This is the most common of the two types. On the right is Ellips l'Archevault, of the longhaired variety. The hair on this dog is characteristically long and slightly wavy. The coat can be any colour.

CHINESE CRESTED DOG

The origins of the Chinese Crested Dog remain a mystery. We only know that it was brought to the United States in the nineteenth century by sailors aboard an American ship arriving from China. The dog owes its name to the toupet-like fur on its head and the fact that the ship came from China. There are two types.

POWDERPUFF WITH VEIL COAT

This dog's shape is identical to the hairless variety, but it is covered with a silky coat that resembles a powder puff. Right: Gi'Yana du Gué de Launay, owned by Mrs. Isabelle Arnoult.

HAIRLESS

Svelte and finely boned, this active graceful dog is 11 to 13 inches tall and weighs a maximum of 10 pounds. The body is completely hairless except for the head, the paws and the end of the tail. The skin can be either mottled or uniformly coloured. A tuft of hair, characterizing the breed, begins at the end of the muzzle and ends at the top of the neck. When he took Gipez Kumar to the 1992 French Farm Show, Mr. Daniel Arnoult was dumbfounded to hear a visitor exclaim: "Look at that dog! What is the world coming to when a dog is sheared like a sheep?" This remark surprised him so much that he thought he'd see what it felt like to be as naked in public as these dogs are (right).

SHIH TZU

Created in the seventeenth century at the Imperial Court of China, the Shih Tzu is a cross between the Lhasa Apso, a gift from the Dalai Lama, and the Peking Spaniel. The breed was maintained by the empresses of China until 1908. The dog is usually between 9 and 11 inches tall. The head is large and round, and the eyes are sombre looking. The head is adorned with a bushy moustache and beard, which are often groomed in the form of a clump of fur that dangles like a chrysanthemum. The fur is very thick and covers the whole body. It is usually long and straight and forms, at the tail, a long plume that is shaped like "the handle on a tea pot". This is a clean, active, well-adjusted and impish companion.

LHASA APSO

The Lhasa probably descends, in part at least, from the Tibetan Spaniel. Experts say that the Lhasa occupied a privileged place in the Tibetan monasteries because it could detect any suspicious sound due to its keen sense of hearing. This small dog is much longer than it is tall. Its head is adorned with a thick beard and moustache. The coat is either uniformly coloured or multicoloured, ranging from white to black, although yellow and brown are the most common colours. Chakparis Calypso's coat is reddish brown. Mrs. Laurent spent years finding a Lhasa of this colour. Robust, friendly and active, this dog loves company and is extremely clean. The Tibetans appreciate the dog for its mountaineering instinct and even claim it can warn of impending avalanches.

ABOVE: Dolmo du Domaine de Monderlay, Shih Tzu, owned by Mrs. Huaux.

TIBETAN SPANIEL

This is one of the oldest of all dog breeds. It is descended from a primitive Asiatic spaniel, which was the predecessor of almost all of the small-sized Asiatic breeds. English breeders developed an interest in the dog during the period between the two World Wars. This is a small dog, about 10 inches high, weighing between 9 and 13 pounds. The body is slightly longer than it is tall. It carries its little head high. Its muzzle is truncated close to the face, and its ears are tufted and dangle around the head. The silky fur is medium long on the body and long on the hindquarters and tail. The backs of the paws are also well tufted. The coat can be any colour. Right: pictured with Germain Gora are Djetjun de la Garde Adhémar, Florette des Yomainris (seated on top of Germain), Hazan and Hangzou des Yomainris (seated next to Germain).

TIBETAN TERRIER

The ancestors of this robust dog, which measures 15 to 16 inches tall, accompanied Tibetan lamas and Yak herders in the mountains. They also accompanied Asian nomads as they travelled towards Europe, thereby becoming the ancestors of several European shepherd breeds, including the Pyrenean shepherd. The Tibetan Terrier is muscular, stocky and has a powerful body. The fur is long and fine, sometimes wavy, and forms a lavish coat that can be any colour except brown. It is friendly and spirited, especially with people it knows. This well-balanced breed is noted for its intelligence. On the other hand, the dog is mistrustful of strangers and quick to alert its master when it hears anything suspicious.

ABOVE: Ardgowing Damelsa, Tibetan Terrier, owned by Mrs. Round Vanlaer.

The Dalmatian is probably the result of a mix between the bull terrier and the pointer. The dog was employed in teams and accompanied the horses and coaches that were used in the past for transportation. The invention of the automobile led to a decline in popularity of this "coach dog," but it made something of a comeback after World War II, mainly because of the incredible popularity of the film *101 Dalmatians.* This is a medium-sized, active and muscular dog. Its long powerful muzzle is offset by floppy ears that hang around the head. The dog has the broad chest of an endurance runner. The tail is slightly curved toward the body. The fur is short, stiff and shiny. The coat is white and notable for its well-defined spots, which that can be either black or brown.

Loyalty, patience and an easygoing temperament are the hallmarks of this breed. Mrs. France Le Mouël describes Dusty de la Mare aux Buis' behaviour accordingly: "To live with a Dalmatian is to live with an aristocrat dressed in a robe of unparalleled beauty. This kindhearted but stubborn animal is more human than dog and it is the best of companions."

CAVALIER KING CHARLES SPANIEL

A very ancient breed, this dog was enormously popular in European courts. The name "King Charles" comes from the fact that the dog was a favourite companion of King Charles II of England. The breed's physiognomy was altered in the nineteenth century and the original breed disappeared. After World War I, breeders attempted to create dogs that looked like the miniature spaniels depicted beside Charles II in paintings. They succeeded, and the new breed was dubbed the "Cavalier King Charles Spaniel." The head is almost flat between the ears, the forehead is somewhat accentuated, the muzzle is tapered and the jaws are strong and perfectly articulated. The senses of sight and smell are particularly well developed in this breed. The dog has a friendly disposition. With an outgoing, adventurous personality, it is afraid of nothing.

KING CHARLES SPANIEL

In the late nineteenth century, English breeders decided that the enormous popularity of the pug was due to its flat muzzle and it took them thirty years to develop a variety with a flattened muzzle. The head is large and round, while the muzzle is square, very short and snubbed. The long pendulous ears are fringed, an essential characteristic of the breed. The dog measures 9 to 12 inches tall and weighs 8 to 14 pounds. Its long silky coat can be black and tan or might include colours referred to as "blenheim" (rich chestnut markings on a pearly white background) or "ruby" (pearly white with bright brownish streaks). The King Charles Spaniel hates solitude. A refined dog, it can display a great deal of dignity when necessary. Right: Tudormurst Royal Falcon and Dear Emma de Vilfloriane, with Mrs. Sylvie Desserne, who is holding a younger King Charles in her arms.

ABOVE: Lillico Mulligan, Cavalier King Charles Spaniel, owned by Mrs. Wendy Lhote.

JAPANESE CHIN

Intelligent and gentle, this dog loves children and family life. Their ancestors originated in Korea and arrived in Japan during the eighth century. Ownership of the dog was restricted to Japanese nobles, and the breed was deliberately limited in order to preserve its rarity. The Japanese Spaniel is a very small dog that is normally about 10 inches high. The coat is lavish and made of long silky fur that covers the entire body except for the muzzle. The long coat contributes wonderfully to the magnificent profile of this animal. Its head is rather large and its small, floppy ears are triangular in shape and set wide apart. The tail is carried above the back. The breed consists of two types that are distinguishable only by a difference in weight: one variety is less than 8 pounds while the other is between 8 and 13 pounds. The coats of both are either brown and white or black and white.

PEKINGESE

This breed originated in China at the time of Confucius and was largely confined to the imperial palace. In 1860, during the sack of Peking, British soldiers captured four Pekingese, took them to England. This is a small, well-proportioned and robust dog that weighs between 6$\frac{1}{2}$ and 11 pounds. The head is very large, flat and broad. The ears are long, floppy and fringed. The eyes are large and dark brown, and the muzzle is wrinkled, very short and very wide. The coat is opulent and can be almost any colour except white and brown. The dog is by nature loyal and gentle, and conceals a fiery temper beneath a calm, almost haughty exterior. Right: Elie Beau Fou Chinn, Genesim Woodoo Lilly, Butterfly and Thalassa du Jardin de Trèfles (top), and Horn's Black Bird and Clémentine du Jardin de Trèfles, seen here in the arms of Mr. and Mrs. Dessauvages.

CONTINENTAL TOY SPANIELS

It was in Flanders that the first traces of this breed appeared in the fourteenth century. The dog was used for hunting back then. During the Renaissance, however, the breed became popular as a lapdog among the ladies of the courts of Europe. They appreciated its mischievous-looking face and its floppy ears. In France, the breed fell out of favour during the eighteenth century but was maintained in Belgium, where breeders developed a straight-eared variety. Today, the different lines are considered to be a single breed that is recognized as both French and Belgian in origin. Robust and well-proportioned, the Continental Toy Spaniel has a fine expressive head, a body that is barely longer than it is tall, straight paws and a plumed tail that it carries above its back. The dog measures a maximum of 11 inches high and weighs between 4 and 11 pounds. The coat is coloured white and tinted either black or fawn.

PAPILLON SPANIEL (WITH ERECT EARS)

Pepejas Zantussa and Sovereign Torndals, as well as their two puppies, Gold and Gary, seen here in the arms of Mr. and Mrs. Jean-Claude Maimberte, all have the surname "les Rouennaises du Petit Couronne". Their ears are erect and open, a trait typical of this version of the Continental Toy Spaniel.

PHALÈNE SPANIEL (WITH DROOPING EARS)

The Phalène Spaniel is characterized by its thin, droopy ears.

ABOVE: Eden dès Perles du Clos, Phalène Spaniel, owned by Miss Sandrine Yonnet.

BOSTON TERRIER

This dog is descended from diverse breeds that were raised for organized dog fights throughout Europe and the United States in the early nineteenth century. In order to lighten the heavy-set bulldog, breeders crossed it with terriers. One of the resulting lines was brought to the United States, where it was crossed again with another breed, a mix between the bulldog and other terriers. The breeders were from the Boston area, hence its name. This dog has a large head, short, square muzzle and small, well-kept ears. The hindquarters are round and the tail is straight. The coat is made of short, very fine and brilliant fur and coloured black and white. The dog has a gracious and powerful gait, which give it a decisive allure. The dog is not aggressive but knows how to make its presence felt and never hesitates to intervene if it feels its master is in danger.

FRENCH BULLDOG

This breed was created in Paris around 1850 by aficionados of small breeds. The dog was especially popular with butchers, and was referred to for many yeras as the "butcher's dog". It is easily recognizable by its small size, large, square head, short, pug-nosed face, and powerful, compact body. The coat is made of fur that is short, tight, shiny and soft. There are two types: one with a black and red (and sometimes white) coat, the other white with black spots. Seen here beside Claire Jacquet, and vigilant as ever, is Enny Idofe de Livandy, known as Etienne. His attitude is characteristic of French bulldogs, who are devoted to their masters, very affec-tionate and extremely pro-tective of children.

ABOVE: Tel The French Connection at Donmar, Boston Terrier, owned by Mr. Laurent Carniaux.

PUG

In the sixteenth century, Dutch sailors brought the dog back from China, where it was known to the Chinese as the "Paï". William III of Orange brought the dog with him to England when he was crowned sovereign in 1689. This is a small, compact dog with a large, heavy-set and round head. The eyes are large and prominent with a lively expression. The ears are small. The tail is rolled up tight on the hindquarters, and the coat is silver, apricot, beige or black. Its black face earned the dog the nickname of "Carlin" in France and Italy in honor of a popular eighteenth-century Italian actor whose first name was Carlo, and who was famous for the black mask he always wore on stage. The Germans and the Dutch call the dog "Mops" (wrathful) due to its fierce-looking head. The pug, however, is a friendly, outgoing dog who loves to play. The English name "pug" comes from the dog's small size. Right: Cupidon del Sol Lleban, with Mr. and Mrs. Beretta.

Sight Hounds

The ancestors of this category of dog first appeared on the wide open steppes of Asia and in the vast deserts of the Middle East and Africa. To feed themselves, they had to hunt in the open and rely on their keen sense of vision, speed and size when pursuing their prey. Their descendants inherited the physical characteristics necessary for speed, endurance and agility. In general, they are svelte and lithe, with a tapered muzzle that gives them an elegant, distinguished appearance. These formidable hunting dogs have always inspired awe and admiration. The kings of France maintained impressive teams of these dogs, which they used when hunting in the forests around Paris and in the Loire Valley. But every coin has a flip side: the remarkable talent these dogs had for hunting resulted in various breeds being banned from it, as they were growing over-zealous and hunting in inappropriate situations. In order to maintain the appealing qualities of these breeds, dog lovers invented alternative activities to occupy the dogs. Thus was born the sport of dog racing, which takes place either on a flat track in a stadium or in an arena with a varied terrain to challenge the dog's hunting abilities. In the latter case, a decoy is dragged across the arena in a zig-zag pattern to imitate an actual wild hare as it is being chased. The development of these sports necessitated a deeper knowledge about the characteristics and behaviour of each of the breeds. The racing associations and breeders carefully codified and selected the more fit specimens in order to further develop their racing abilities. Consequently, the races themselves have become an essential tool for perpetuating those breeds used in competition. All these dogs are marked by a sense of independence and prudence. As powerful athletes, they need a lot of exercise.

AFGHAN HOUND

This is a very ancient breed from a little known region of the world. The breed has not changed much over time. For many years, Afghanistan restricted exports—these were so successful that the first Afghan was not introduced into Britain until 1907. The breed did not appear in France until 1930. The dog stands 24 to 30 inches tall and has an impressive, dignified carriage. Eve U'zlo d'Ahmadâbâd, seen here with Miss Christine Soliveau, epitomizes the accentuated features of the breed with his proud disposition, intelligent expression and haughty allure. The sumptuous fur of the Afghan is composed of long, silky hair on the head, paws and sides. The fur on the back, on the other hand, is short and stiff and forms a sort of saddle. The tail is fringed and bow-shaped. The coat can be any colour. Proud and independent, the Afghan has retained its instincts as a hunter and its remarkable abilities as a runner.

HUNGARIAN GREYHOUND

The Hungarian Greyhound has ancient Asiatic origins. It came to Europe with the first Magyars who settled near the Carpathian mountains in the ninth century. It was crossed with other greyhound breeds in the nineteenth century to enhance its speed and agility. Less elongated than the standard greyhound, this dog also has a longer and more curved tail. The dog is about 28 inches tall, and the head is triangular in shape. The ears are of medium length and floppy. The neck is muscular, and the back is straight. The coat is composed of short fur and is slightly rough. The colour of the coat can vary and is either uniformly spotted or even striped.

362

ABOVE: Vera Arpadhazi, Hungarian Greyhound, owned by Mr. Christophe Carrier.

ARABIAN GREYHOUND

The Arabian greyhound, which descended from a primitive Asiatic, was introduced into North Africa in the seventeenth century. The development of the breed was rather haphazard at first, but a more homogenous line emerged with breeders who belonged to nomadic tribes. Measuring 26 to 30 inches tall and weighing an average of 66 pounds, this dog has an elongated and elegant head. The back is short and almost horizontal, and the tail is very thin. The coat is so fine that the dog's wiry body is readily apparent. This quality is especially visible in D'Selma (far right). Her aloofness might make you think that she prefers to ignore Mrs. Renée Lagrange, but this is hardly the case. Despite the seemingly haughty personality, this dog gets very attached to its masters, and albeit subtly, D'Selma is watching Mrs. Lagrange and is ready at all times to obey her every command.

SALUKI

This dog's ancestors were the large primitive Asiatic greyhounds that inhabited Central Asia some 10,000 years ago. The British discovered this dog in the late nineteenth century and started breeding it in the early twentieth century. Breeding began in France after World War II. The Saluki is 24 to 28 inches tall and weighs between 33 and 66 pounds. It has the perfect build for hunting. The elongated head features large floppy ears covered with silky fur. The tail is long and well-furnished with tassels. The coat is smooth and soft and can be white, beige, golden, red, gray and tan, black and tan, or black, white and tan. This is a faithful, friendly and dignified dog.

ABOVE: Bloody Grizzly de Cassandra, Saluki, owned by Miss Claudine Boyaval.

What an incredible impression Epahaistos of Leanan Sidhe and Dew of Leanan Sidhe (right) make. Mr. Bridier's dogs epitomize the perfectly controlled power of this breed. But also note their serenity and gentleness. The breed is descended from wire-haired Continental greyhounds that date to the early Christian era. From the tenth to the seventeenth centuries, the Irish Wolfhound was used to hunt wolves. Standing 36 inches tall and weighing around 175 pounds, this is, along with the Great Dane, the largest dog breed. These dogs are strongly built and muscular yet agile. The head and tail are carried high. The wiry coat can be grey, red, black or white. This is also a good guard dog, and its imposing size can be very dissuasive.

Mistic-Myth of the Funny Hill, who belongs to Mrs. Duval-Pinset, is a charming companion (following double page). The name Deerhound points to the fact that this large dog (29 inches) descends from primitive greyhounds that accompanied the Celts when they settled in Scotland around 300 BC. This dog was a formidable deerhunter and was perfect for hunting in the forests that cover the Scottish Highlands. The Scottish Deerhound has a long, flat head. The muzzle is narrow and tapered at the nose. The neck is long and the shoulders angular. The long tail hangs straight down when the dog is at rest. The coat is wiry and coarse and about 4 inches long. The coat is longer around the head, the chest and the stomach. It can be grey-blue (the most sought-after color), light grey or spotted grey.

GREYHOUND

This dog's ancestors were primitive greyhounds that arrived with the Celts when they settled in the British Isles. During the Middles Ages, this hunting dog was restricted to the nobility. During the Renaissance, hunting competitions became so popular that certain breeders crossed the greyhound with the bull terrier. It was at this point that the standard breed was established as it exists today. The greyhound is 28 to 30 inches tall. It has a long head and a long tail. Its broad, elevated chest and elongated neck, along with a long, square back account for its harmonious and aerodynamic shape. The fur is tight and fine. The coat can be uniformly black, white, red, blue, or fawn, or it can have any mixture of those colours offset with white. At one time a deerhunting dog, the greyhound has remained to this day an inveterate hunting dog. Its speed and endurance are remarkable. Far right: Danton du Lavoir de Datchet, owned by Mr. Labastrou.

WHIPPET

This small English greyhound has distant origins, despite the fact that its name didn't appear until the nineteenth century. Its defining characteristics were not established until the late nineteenth century when the breed was crossed with fox terriers. The characteristics were further developed following an intensive breeding programme based on the dog's ability to compete in the ever popular dog races. The head is long, with small ears. The chest is considerably elevated; the back is rather wide and long, and the tail is tapered. The fur is short, fine and very tight, and the coat can be any colour.

ABOVE: Oakbark Master Quizz, Whippet, owned by Mr. Alain Olu.

The Romans introduced Celtic greyhounds into Spain, and later the conquering Arabs imported Asiatic greyhounds. The Spanish Greyhound is the product of several crosses between these earlier breeds. After deciding that the breed lacked sufficient speed, it was crossed with the standard greyhound, and the result was the modern Spanish Greyhound. Today, it is used to hunt wild hare in Spain, where the use of greyhounds for hunting is not forbidden. The dog is also used in hunting rabbit and fox. The dog stands 26 to 28 inches tall at the shoulder and weighs around 66 pounds. The head is long, and straight with large nostrils and triangular ears. The back is long, and the stomach is arched. Its long tail ends in a point. The coat can be any colour, but the most common are fawn and brindled or black. The breed is divided into two categories, distinguished by the nature of their coats. The first type has a coarse, semi-long coat, as can be seen on Vasconcico, called Vasco (black), and Vilancico, called Vivaldi (brindled), both of whom belong to Mr. Pierre Faure (right). Having coats typical of the breed, both of these dogs exemplify the breed's excellent balance, which comes from regular exercise and chasing decoys.

Sometime around 3000 B.C., the ancestors of the Italian greyhound enjoyed a privileged place among the Egyptians, who succeeded in miniaturizing a primitive Asiatic greyhound to create the breed. The P.L.I., as the French refer to the dog, was brought to Italy from Egypt and became a favourite among the Italian nobility. It was there that breeding programmes established the modern breed. The search for perfection and refinement that so characterized the Renaissance was applied with equal enthusiasm to the breeding of this dog.

With its small size, the Italian Greyhound is an active and energetic athlete, whose gait is characterised by remarkably long strides. The dog is a model of grace and elegance, but is also a wonderful companion, with an attractive and playful temperament. The head is tapered, and the muzzle is pointed. The ears are small and elegant. Its large eyes are very expressive. The coat is made of short hair that is glossy and soft to the touch, and it can be uniformly colored black, grey, fawn and beige, with a patch of white on the chest or at the end of the paws in some dogs. A track champion, Ever Black de Shirkan and his admiring entourage belong to Mrs. Evelyne Diacquenod, who fondly remembers Ever Black's mother, Belle Bressane de Shirkan. She was a resolutely independent dog who passed by the florist's every day to say hello, after which she would return home for a quick nap. Then she would visit the TV store and the diner to say hello, before stopping at the butcher's where she knew the door would always be open. There she would lie down and wait patiently until Mrs. Diacquenod came to fetch her when the butcher called to say that Belle had arrived. Without even realizing it, Belle Bressane put into practice a sensible and widely employed political dictum: independence through interdependence.

BORZOÏ

The origins of this breed remain controversial, but it seems likely that the lineage of the Borzoï includes diverse Asiatic greyhounds. The breed was more or less established in its modern form in the fifteenth century during the reign of Ivan the Terrible. The original breeders wanted a greyhound that would hunt wolves. That meant a large, strong and fast dog. The Borzoï fit the bill perfectly. The dog can be as tall as 33 inches and has a brilliant, silky, wavy coat that can be white and fawn, white and brindled, or black and white. Its large, sombre, almond-shaped eyes accentuate the noble aspect of its long, chiseled head. Its back forms a long sloping arch, and its long tail is fringed. Over time, this dog has become more of a pet than a hunting dog, yet it still retains many of the qualities for which it was originally bred. When given the opportunity, this dog can be an avid and courageous hunter.

AZAWAKH

This elegant greyhound comes from the plateau of central Mali and was named after the Azawakh river. It arrived there in the eighth century with the people of the Saharas who were moving westward to escape the invading Arabs. The dog is 30 inches tall and has a long, finely-featured head with flat, floppy ears. Its legs are long and thin, the chest is substantial, the back is straight and the tail is thin. The fur is short, fine and soft and forms a coat that varies from sandy white to brown. This breed is generally slender, so much so, that its muscles and bones are readily visible through the coat. Judging by the proud, almost imperial appearance adopted by Casque d'Or des Nomades Bleus, who belongs to Mrs. Françoise Heidmann, it is easy to see why the nomads of the Sahara considered the Azawakh to be an animal of ceremonial and ritual importance.

INDEX

INDEX

INDEX

ACKNOWLEDGEMENTS

I would like to extend special thanks to Sylvie Mignon
of the Central Canine Society
who patiently answered our many questions
concerning dogs and dog owners;
Pierre de Mascureau, Director of the Central Canine Society;
the presidents of all the dog clubs in France
and their supporters,
who are too numerous to mention individually;
the technicians who set up the studio
where the photographs were taken;
the carpenters from Marcel Duperche's firm;
the masons from the firm of Yves Cojean;
the electricians from Flèche and Morin;
and Willy Décor for their work on the interiors.
I would also like to thank my two assistants,
Françoise Jacquot, who took care of scheduling,
and Marc Lavaud, who was responsible for lighting,
as well as Jean-Philippe Piter.

The film was developed in the
GT3P laboratory at Saint-Rémy-l'Honoré.
The negatives were printed for the book by
Rush Labo of Paris,
who also handled the project presentation.
The photographs were made with a Mamiya RZ 67
and a Canon Eos 1 using a Godard flash.
Thanks also to the entire Sotexi team,
particularly Giselle Nicot.
Kodak Ektachrome 100 X.
The photographs are distributed by
Yann Arthus-Bertrand. Fax: +33 (1) 34 86 76 46.